UNIQ Business: Lessons and Strategies from 35 of the Best Business Books

ISBN: See back cover.
Cover design by the UNIQ Agency.
For more information, please visit https://uniq.agency or contact the author directly.
Printed in the United Kingdom.

Get Insights and Results for Your Business, Branding, and Marketing Strategies with the UNIQ Scorecard

Unlock the Potential of Your Business with the Help of the UNIQ Agency

Are you struggling to achieve the growth and success you want for your business? Are you uncertain about the **effectiveness** of your branding and marketing strategies? You're not alone. Many business owners face similar challenges when it comes to developing and executing a winning strategy.

But there's **good news**. With the UNIQ Scorecard, you can get the insights and results you need to unlock the potential of your business. As a leading branding and marketing agency, UNIQ has helped countless businesses like yours achieve their goals and grow their bottom line.

The UNIQ Scorecard is a comprehensive assessment tool that measures the effectiveness of your business, branding, and marketing strategies. With just a few simple questions, you'll **receive scores** for each area and valuable insights into what's working and what's not.

Scan the QR code to take the Scorecard

About the Author

Hi, my name is Nick Eagle, and I am the creative director of UNIQ, a branding agency located in Oxfordshire. Our agency specialises in helping business owners gain the confidence to become market leaders by providing branding and marketing solutions that truly represent their vision and goals.

Before founding UNIQ, I grew a personal training business in the heart of Oxford. While on my entrepreneurial journey, I realised how easy it was to get lost in the day-to-day running of the business. With the overwhelming amount of information available online and in books, it was challenging to find the best techniques for growing my business.

That's when I decided to read dozens of business, marketing, and branding books to learn how to effectively grow my business. I took copious notes on each book, distilling the information down to the key insights and action steps that have helped me grow my business over the past 10 years.

Now, I have compiled those notes into a book that I consider to be a field manual for operating a business and a notebook of all the notes I have taken. It contains summaries of the most important books that have helped me become a successful business owner, with the goal of helping others achieve the same level of success.

This book is not just a list of book summaries, but rather a guidebook on how to grow and market a business. It is the culmination of a decade of learning and practical experience, and it has been designed to help business owners succeed in today's rapidly changing business landscape.

In this book, you will find summaries of the most important books that have helped me in my own journey as a business owner. You will also find practical action steps that you can take to implement the insights and principles into your own business.

My hope is that this book will help you avoid some of the pitfalls that I faced and provide you with the tools and strategies you need to succeed in your business. Whether you are just starting out or have been in business for years, this book will provide valuable insights and practical advice to help you grow and achieve your goals.

I am excited to share this book with you and look forward to hearing about your success as you implement the principles and strategies outlined in its pages. Let's grow and succeed together!

UNIQ Business: Lessons and Strategies from 30 of the Best Business Books

Introduction

Welcome to UNIQ Business: Lessons and Strategies from 35 of the Best Business Books. This book is a comprehensive guide for entrepreneurs and business owners seeking to grow their businesses, build their brands, and develop their marketing strategies.

This book is best suited for entrepreneurs and business owners who want to learn quickly about business, branding and marketing and who are looking for actionable strategies to take their businesses to the next level. Whether you are a seasoned entrepreneur or just starting out, this book provides insights, practical advice, and key summaries of the most important books I have read that can help you grow your business.

The book is designed to be read in any order that suits your needs. You can start by focusing on the topics that are most relevant to your current situation, or you can read the book cover-to-cover to gain a comprehensive understanding of business from some of the best books written.

The book is organised to provide you with the key insights and action steps from each book I have taken notes on over the past 10 years. It is meant to be a book that becomes your business partner over the years, something you always refer to for guidance and answers. Helping you to find answers to key business questions when needed.

You will learn how to build a strong brand, develop marketing strategies that resonate with your target audience, and effectively promote your products or services.

My goal in creating this book is to provide entrepreneurs and business owners with a single resource they can turn to for guidance, inspiration, and practical advice. This book distils the most important concepts from dozens of books, making it an invaluable resource for those seeking to grow and succeed in the world of business.

So, whether you are starting a new business or looking to grow an existing one; this book is a must-read. I hope it will help you achieve your goals, inspire you and give you the confidence to go and become a market leader.

"The Lean Startup" by Eric Ries:

This book is a must-read for anyone interested in starting their own business or working in a startup. It provides a practical guide for creating a successful, innovative company.

Key Takeaway

The Lean Startup philosophy encourages a focus on continuous learning and experimentation, rather than executing a predetermined plan, to reduce the risk of failure and increase the chances of success.

As a business owner, I'm always looking for ways to improve my company's efficiency and profitability. That's why I found "The Lean Startup" by Eric Ries to be such an insightful and practical guide to creating a successful business in today's fast-paced and unpredictable market.

Philosophy of the Lean Startup

The Lean Startup is a philosophy that encourages businesses to focus on continuous learning and experimentation, rather than executing a predetermined plan. This approach is particularly useful in today's fast-changing and unpredictable market, where traditional methods of product development and business planning may not be effective.

The main philosophy of the Lean Startup is to focus on the development of a Minimum Viable Product (MVP) and then gather feedback from customers to improve and iterate on that product. This iterative process of experimentation and learning is at the core of the Lean Startup philosophy.

Key Takeaways

The Lean Startup philosophy provides several key takeaways for businesses of any size, including:

1. Start with the MVP: Instead of spending months or years developing a product, entrepreneurs should focus on creating a minimum viable product (MVP) that can be quickly tested and improved based on customer feedback. The MVP is not intended to be perfect, but rather to provide a starting point for experimentation and learning.

2. Use validated learning: In order to improve the MVP, entrepreneurs should focus on validated learning, which involves testing hypotheses and assumptions with real customers to see if they hold up. By collecting data and feedback from customers, entrepreneurs can make informed decisions about what changes to make to the product.

3. Pivot when necessary: If the data and feedback suggest that the current approach is not working, entrepreneurs should be willing to pivot and change course. This can be a difficult decision, but it

is often necessary in order to create a successful product and business.

4. Embrace the uncertainty: Starting a business is inherently uncertain, and entrepreneurs should embrace that uncertainty rather than trying to eliminate it. By focusing on learning and experimentation, entrepreneurs can reduce the risk of failure and increase their chances of success.

Action Steps

Implementing the Lean Startup philosophy can be challenging, but there are several action steps that business owners can take to get started.

1. Identify the MVP: Start by identifying the minimum viable product that can be quickly developed and tested. This might involve creating a prototype or a simplified version of the product.

2. Test with real customers: Once the MVP has been developed, test it with real customers to gather feedback and data. This might involve creating a landing page, running a small-scale test, or conducting customer interviews.

3. Use data to make informed decisions: Use the data and feedback gathered from customers to make informed decisions about what changes to make to the product. This might involve tweaking the design, adding or removing features, or changing the

pricing.

4. Iterate and pivot: Based on the data and feedback, iterate on the MVP to create an improved version. If the data suggests that the current approach is not working, be willing to pivot and change course.

5. Embrace the uncertainty: Remember that starting a business is inherently uncertain, and embrace that uncertainty. Focus on learning and experimentation, and be willing to make mistakes and learn from them.

Conclusion

In conclusion, "The Lean Startup" by Eric Ries is a groundbreaking book that challenges the traditional approach to entrepreneurship and provides a roadmap for building a successful business in a rapidly changing marketplace. By emphasising the importance of testing assumptions, creating a culture of innovation, and using data to guide decision-making, Ries shows us how to become more agile and adaptive in a constantly evolving business landscape. As business owners, implementing the insights and action steps from this book can help us to identify potential opportunities, create a culture of experimentation, and take calculated risks to stay ahead of the competition.

"The Lean Startup" is a must-read for anyone looking to start a new business or improve an existing one, as it provides practical guidance on how to build a scalable and sustainable enterprise that can thrive in the long-term.

"The Brand Flip" by Marty Neumeier

The Brand Flip by Marty Neumeier is a book that explores the changing landscape of branding and how businesses must adapt in order to thrive in the digital age.

The book argues that traditional branding strategies are no longer effective, and that businesses must embrace a new approach to branding that is more agile, customer-focused, and authentic. In this chapter summary, I will provide an overview of the book, highlight its main philosophy and key takeaways, and provide actionable steps that a business owner can take to implement these ideas.

The Brand Flip was first published in 2015 and has since become a popular resource for anyone looking to understand the changing landscape of branding. The book is divided into two parts. Part One provides an introduction to the concept of the brand flip and why it is important for businesses to adapt. Part Two explores the practical aspects of the brand flip, including developing a brand strategy, creating a brand identity, and implementing a brand experience.

Main Philosophy

At the heart of Neumeier's philosophy is the idea that businesses must embrace a new approach to branding in order to succeed in the digital age. The traditional approach to branding, which focused on creating a consistent, polished image, is no longer effective. Instead, businesses must embrace a new approach that is more agile, customer-focused, and authentic.

The brand flip is the process of flipping the traditional approach to branding on its head. Instead of focusing on creating a consistent image, businesses must focus on creating a consistent experience for customers. This means developing a brand strategy that is focused on customer needs and desires, creating a brand identity that is authentic and resonates with customers, and implementing a brand experience that is consistent across all touchpoints.

Key Takeaways

1. Focus on customer needs and desires: The traditional approach to branding is no longer effective. Instead, businesses must focus on customer needs and desires in order to develop a brand strategy that resonates with customers.

2. Be authentic: In the digital age, authenticity is more important than ever. Businesses must be authentic and transparent in their branding in order to build trust with customers.

3. Develop a brand experience: The brand experience is the sum total of all customer interactions with your brand. Businesses must

focus on creating a consistent and memorable brand experience across all touchpoints.

4. Embrace agility: In the digital age, businesses must be agile and adaptable in order to respond to changing customer needs and market conditions.

5. Build a community: In the digital age, building a community around your brand is essential. Businesses should focus on building a community of engaged customers who are passionate about their products or services.

Action Steps for Business Owners

Focus on customer needs and desires

Spend time understanding the needs and desires of your customers. Use customer research and feedback to inform your brand strategy and create a brand that resonates with your target audience.

Be authentic

Be authentic and transparent in your branding. Don't try to be something that you're not, as customers will see through this and it will damage your credibility.

Develop a brand experience

Focus on creating a consistent and memorable brand experience across all touchpoints. This includes your website, social media, advertising, and customer interactions.

Embrace agility

Embrace agility and adaptability in order to respond to changing customer needs and market conditions. Be willing to pivot your branding strategy when necessary in order to stay relevant.

Build a community

Build a community of engaged customers who are passionate about your products or services. Encourage customers to share their experiences with your brand on social media and other platforms, and provide opportunities for customers to engage with your brand and each other.

Create a brand strategy

Develop a brand strategy that is focused on customer needs and desires. Identify your target audience, their pain points and desires, and develop a messaging strategy that speaks directly to them.

Develop a brand identity

Develop a brand identity that is authentic and resonates with your target audience. This includes your brand name, logo, and visual identity.

Implement a brand experience

Implement a brand experience that is consistent and memorable across all touchpoints. This includes your website, social media, advertising, and customer interactions.

Monitor and adjust

Monitor the effectiveness of your branding strategy and adjust it as needed. Use data and analytics to track the performance of your branding efforts and make adjustments when necessary.

Foster a culture of innovation

Foster a culture of innovation within your business by encouraging employees to take risks and try new things. Reward employees who come up with innovative ideas and provide resources and support to help them bring their ideas to life.

Conclusion

The Brand Flip by Marty Neumeier provides a practical and actionable framework for developing a brand strategy that is focused on customer needs and desires. By embracing authenticity, focusing on the customer experience, and being agile and adaptable, businesses can succeed in the digital age. By developing a brand strategy that speaks directly to their target audience, creating a brand identity that is authentic and resonates with customers, and implementing a brand experience that is consistent and memorable across all touchpoints, businesses can build a strong and loyal customer base.

By fostering a culture of innovation and monitoring the effectiveness of their branding efforts, businesses can stay ahead of the competition and drive business success.

"The Key Person of Influence" by Daniel Priestley

The Key Person of Influence by Daniel Priestley is a book that explores the concept of becoming a key person of influence in your industry.

The book argues that in order to succeed in the modern economy, individuals must establish themselves as key influencers in their industry. In this chapter summary, I will provide an overview of the book, highlight its main philosophy and key takeaways, and provide actionable steps that a business owner can take to implement these ideas.

The Key Person of Influence was first published in 2010 and has since become a popular resource for anyone looking to establish themselves as a key influencer in their industry. The book is divided into five sections, each of which explores a different aspect of becoming a key person of influence. The sections are illustrated with real-world examples and practical advice for how to build influence and establish yourself as a thought leader in your industry.

Main Philosophy

At the heart of Priestley's philosophy is the idea that individuals must establish themselves as key influencers in their industry in order to succeed in the modern economy. This requires a combination of knowledge, skills, and personal branding. By establishing themselves as thought leaders and building a personal brand, individuals can create new opportunities for themselves, build a loyal following, and establish themselves as key influencers in their industry.

Key Takeaways

1. Develop a niche: In order to become a key person of influence, it's important to develop a niche within your industry. This means identifying a specific area of expertise that sets you apart from others in your field.

2. Build your personal brand: In order to establish yourself as a key influencer, you must build a strong personal brand. This means developing a clear and consistent message and image across all of your online and offline platforms.

3. Establish thought leadership: In order to establish yourself as a key influencer, you must establish yourself as a thought leader in your industry. This means producing high-quality content that showcases your knowledge and expertise.

4. Build a network: In order to build influence, it's important to build a strong network of contacts within your industry. This means attending industry events, building relationships with influencers, and collaborating with other thought leaders.

5. Be a person of influence: In order to become a key person of influence, you must be a person of influence. This means being a positive and influential force in your industry, building trust with your audience, and being a thought leader and innovator.

Action Steps for Business Owners

Develop a niche
Spend time identifying a specific area of expertise that sets you apart from others in your field. This could be a particular skill set, a unique approach to a common problem, or a specific market segment that you are particularly knowledgeable about.

Build your personal brand
Develop a clear and consistent message and image across all of your online and offline platforms. This includes your website, social media, business cards, and any other materials that you use to represent your brand.

Establish thought leadership
Produce high-quality content that showcases your knowledge and expertise. This could include blog posts, podcasts, videos, webinars, or any other format that is relevant to your industry.

Build a network

Attend industry events, build relationships with influencers, and collaborate with other thought leaders. This could include participating in online communities, attending conferences and trade shows, or joining industry groups and associations.
Be a person of influence: Build trust with your audience by being a positive and influential force in your industry. Be a thought leader and innovator, and work to solve common problems within your industry.

Build a team

Build a team of like-minded individuals who share your vision and can help you achieve your goals. This could include partners, employees, or freelancers who can help you produce content, market your brand, and build your network.

Continuously learn and develop your skills

Continuously learn and develop your skills in order to stay relevant and ahead of the curve. This means attending training and development opportunities, reading industry publications, and staying up-to-date on the latest trends and innovations in your industry.

Be persistent

Establishing yourself as a key person of influence takes time and persistence. Don't get discouraged if you don't see immediate results. Stay committed to your goals and continue to put in the effort required to build your influence.

Focus on providing value

Focus on providing value to your audience and building relationships with them. This means being generous with your time and knowledge, and focusing on how you can help others rather than what you can gain for yourself.

Measure your progress

Measure the progress you are making in building your influence. Use data and analytics to track the performance of your content, your social media engagement, and your overall influence within your industry.

Conclusion

The Key Person of Influence by Daniel Priestley provides a practical and actionable framework for becoming a key influencer in your industry. By developing a niche, building a strong personal brand, establishing thought leadership, building a network, and being a person of influence, individuals can create new opportunities for themselves and establish themselves as thought leaders in their industry.

By building a team, continuously learning and developing their skills, being persistent, and focusing on providing value, individuals can build a loyal following and establish themselves as key influencers in their industry.

By measuring their progress and staying committed to their goals, individuals can achieve success and build a successful and fulfilling career as a key person of influence.

"Legacy" by James Kerr

Legacy by James Kerr is a book that explores the leadership philosophy of the New Zealand All Blacks rugby team, one of the most successful sports teams in history.

The book argues that the All Blacks' success is due to a unique leadership approach that emphasises the importance of team culture, personal accountability, and continuous improvement. In this chapter summary, I will provide an overview of the book, highlight its main philosophy and key takeaways, and provide actionable steps that a business owner can take to implement these ideas.

Legacy was first published in 2013 and has since become a popular resource for anyone looking to understand the leadership philosophy of the All Blacks rugby team. The book is divided into 15 chapters, each of which explores a different aspect of the team's culture and leadership approach. The chapters are illustrated with real-world examples and practical advice for how to apply these principles to business and life.

Main Philosophy

At the heart of Kerr's philosophy is the idea that great leaders build great teams by creating a culture of excellence. This means establishing a clear set of values, setting high standards for performance, and creating a sense of personal accountability within the team. The All Blacks' success is due to their unique leadership approach, which emphasises the importance of team culture, personal accountability, and continuous improvement.

Key Takeaways

1. Embrace a strong team culture: The All Blacks' success is due in large part to their strong team culture. This means establishing a clear set of values, developing a sense of belonging within the team, and creating a strong team identity.

2. Set high standards: The All Blacks set the bar high for performance and hold themselves to a higher standard than their competitors. This means focusing on the small details and constantly striving for improvement.

3. Foster personal accountability: The All Blacks encourage personal accountability by setting clear expectations, promoting self-reflection, and encouraging team members to take ownership of their roles and responsibilities.

4. Focus on continuous improvement: The All Blacks have a culture of continuous improvement, constantly seeking out ways to learn and grow as individuals and as a team. This means encouraging experimentation and taking risks, and being willing

to learn from mistakes.

Action Steps for Business Owners

Establish a strong team culture
Develop a clear set of values that align with your business goals and establish a strong team identity. Encourage team members to embrace these values and create a sense of belonging within the team.

Set high standards
Set the bar high for performance and hold yourself and your team to a higher standard than your competitors. Focus on the small details and constantly seek out ways to improve your products or services.

Foster personal accountability
Encourage personal accountability by setting clear expectations and encouraging team members to take ownership of their roles and responsibilities. Promote self-reflection and encourage team members to learn from their mistakes.

Focus on continuous improvement

Foster a culture of continuous improvement by encouraging experimentation and taking risks. Provide opportunities for team members to learn and grow, and be willing to learn from your own mistakes.

Build a strong team

Build a strong team by hiring individuals who align with your values and goals, and creating a sense of belonging within the team. Encourage collaboration and communication, and build strong relationships with team members.

Develop strong leadership

Develop strong leadership by leading by example and modelling the behaviour you want to see in your team. Set clear expectations and provide feedback and coaching to help team members improve.

Embrace diversity

Embrace diversity within your team and encourage different perspectives and ideas. Create a culture of inclusivity that welcomes and values differences.

Promote innovation

Promote innovation by encouraging creativity and

experimentation. Create a culture of curiosity and be willing to try new things.

Build resilience

Build resilience by promoting mental and physical health within your team. Encourage team members to take care of themselves and support them when they face challenges or setbacks.

Focus on the long-term

Focus on the long-term success of your business by setting clear goals and developing a plan to achieve them. Be willing to make short-term sacrifices in order to achieve long-term success.

Conclusion

Legacy by James Kerr provides a powerful and inspiring framework for building a successful team culture based on the leadership philosophy of the New Zealand All Blacks rugby team. By embracing a strong team culture, setting high standards, fostering personal accountability, and focusing on continuous improvement, businesses can achieve success and build a strong and loyal following.

By building a strong team, developing strong leadership, embracing diversity, promoting innovation, building resilience, and focusing on the long-term success of the business, businesses can create a culture of excellence that drives success and creates a legacy for future generations.

By embracing these principles and applying them to their own businesses, business owners can achieve success and build a business that lasts for generations.

Take Your Shot - Robin Waite

In Robin Waite's book, "Take Your Shot: How to Grow Your Business, Attract More Clients, and Make More Money," he emphasises the importance of taking action, being bold, and making the most of every opportunity.

Throughout the book, Robin uses real-world examples and case studies to illustrate his points and provide inspiration for readers. For example, he tells the story of a Golf Professional who was struggling to grow his business, but was able to turn things around by taking bold action and making changes to his marketing strategy.

In addition, Robin Waite draws on his own experience as a business coach and consultant, sharing insights throughout the story format. This helps to make the book feel more personal and relatable, as readers can see how the ideas and advice presented in the book can work in real-world situations.

Philosophy

At the heart of "Take Your Shot" is the philosophy that business success requires action. Robin Waite argues that too many business owners focus on strategy and planning, but fail to take action. He believes that without action, even the best-laid plans are worthless.

To succeed in business, he believes that you must be bold, take risks, and seize every opportunity that comes your way. This philosophy is based on the idea that you should not wait for the perfect moment to take action. Instead, you should take action as soon as possible, and make adjustments along the way.

Key Takeaways

Take Action

The most important takeaway from "Take Your Shot" is that you must take action. Waite emphasises the importance of taking action, even if you don't feel ready or don't have all the answers. He believes that taking action is the only way to move your business forward.

Action Step

Take action on one thing you have been putting off today. It can be a small task or a larger project, but the key is to take action and get started.

Focus on the Right Things

Another key takeaway from "Take Your Shot" is the importance of focusing on the right things. Waite argues that too many business owners waste their time and energy on tasks that don't move their business forward.

Instead, he recommends focusing on the things that will have the biggest impact on your business. This includes things like marketing, sales, and customer service.

Action Step
Identify the top three things that will have the biggest impact on your business and focus on those things every day.

Be Bold
To succeed in business, Waite believes that you must be bold. This means taking risks, being willing to fail, and stepping outside of your comfort zone.
Waite argues that being bold is essential for growth and success. If you're not willing to take risks and try new things, you'll never achieve your full potential.

Action Step
Identify one area where you can be bolder in your business. This could be trying a new marketing strategy, reaching out to a potential client, or launching a new product.

Build Relationships

In "Take Your Shot," Waite emphasises the importance of building relationships. He argues that the success of your business is heavily dependent on the relationships you build with your customers, employees, and partners.

To build strong relationships, Waite recommends focusing on empathy, communication, and trust. He believes that if you can build strong relationships with the people in your business, you'll be more likely to succeed.

Action Step

Schedule time each week to connect with your customers, employees, or partners. This could be a phone call, a meeting, or simply sending a quick email to check in.

Embrace Failure

Finally, Waite believes that it's important to embrace failure. He argues that failure is an essential part of growth and success, and that you should not be afraid to fail.

Waite believes that if you're not failing, you're not trying hard enough. He encourages business owners to embrace failure, learn from their mistakes, and use those experiences to grow and improve.

Action Step

Identify one recent failure or mistake in your business and reflect on what you learned from it.

Conclusion

In conclusion, "Take Your Shot" is a valuable resource for business owners who are looking to take their business to the next level. By focusing on the importance of action, boldness, and relationships, Waite provides a roadmap for success that is both practical and motivational.

Whether you're a startup or an established business, "Take Your Shot" can help you achieve your goals and take your business to new heights.

"Good to Great" by Jim Collins:

This book explores what sets successful companies apart from the rest, and how they sustain their success over the long term.

"Good to Great" by Jim Collins is a bestselling business book that offers a data-driven analysis of what separates successful companies from those that are merely good. The book is based on a five-year research project that analysed the performance of companies over a period of 15 years, comparing those that made the leap from good to great with those that did not. The study aimed to identify the key factors that led to long-term success, and the insights it offers have become essential reading for business owners, entrepreneurs, and leaders.

Philosophy of Good to Great:

The philosophy of "Good to Great" is based on the idea that sustained success comes from a combination of disciplined action, effective leadership, and a culture of excellence. The book argues that truly great companies are those that are able to achieve sustained growth and profitability, and that this can only be achieved by building a strong foundation, investing in the right people, and maintaining a relentless focus on performance.

Key Takeaways:

There are several key takeaways from "Good to Great" that business owners can use to improve their company's performance and achieve long-term success:

1. Start with a strong foundation: Building a strong foundation is essential for achieving long-term success. This means developing a clear vision, establishing a culture of excellence, and creating a system for managing every aspect of the business.

2. Get the right people on the bus: In order to achieve sustained success, companies need to have the right people in the right positions. This means hiring employees who are passionate, driven, and committed to achieving the company's goals.

3. Confront the brutal facts: Successful companies are those that are willing to confront the brutal facts of their situation, rather than relying on wishful thinking or false optimism. This means being realistic about the challenges facing the company, and taking decisive action to address them.

4. Create a culture of discipline: Successful companies are those that maintain a culture of discipline, in which everyone is committed to achieving the company's goals. This means setting clear expectations, maintaining high standards of performance, and holding everyone accountable for their actions.

5. Embrace technology: Companies that are able to harness the

power of technology are those that are best positioned for long-term success. This means investing in technology that can improve productivity, streamline operations, and enhance the customer experience.

Action Steps:

Here are some action steps that business owners can take to implement the insights from "Good to Great" in their own companies:

1. Start with a strong foundation: Develop a clear vision for your company, establish a culture of excellence, and create a system for managing every aspect of the business.

2. Get the right people on the bus: Focus on hiring employees who are passionate, driven, and committed to achieving the company's goals.

3. Confront the brutal facts: Be realistic about the challenges facing your company, and take decisive action to address them.

4. Create a culture of discipline: Set clear expectations, maintain high standards of performance, and hold everyone accountable for their actions.

5. Embrace technology: Invest in technology that can improve productivity, streamline operations, and enhance the customer

experience.

Good is the Enemy of Great

The first chapter of "Good to Great" argues that many companies that are successful at the outset become complacent, and fail to achieve sustained success over the long-term. The book contends that being good is not enough, and that truly great companies are those that are able to make the leap from good to great.

Level 5 Leadership

Chapter 2 introduces the concept of Level 5 Leadership, which is characterised by a combination of personal humility and professional will. The book argues that truly great companies are those that are led by Level 5 Leaders, who are able to inspire and motivate their teams, while also remaining grounded and humble.

First Who, Then What

Chapter 3 focuses on the importance of getting the right people on the bus. The book argues that the most successful companies are those that are able to identify and hire the right employees, based on their skills, passion, and commitment to the company's vision and values.

Confront the Brutal Facts

Chapter 4 emphasises the importance of being realistic about the challenges facing your company, and taking decisive action to address them. The book argues that successful companies are those that are able to confront the brutal facts of their situation, and make tough decisions when necessary.

The Hedgehog Concept

Chapter 5 introduces the concept of the Hedgehog Concept, which is based on the idea that the most successful companies are those that focus on a specific area of expertise, and become the best in the world at that particular thing. The book argues that companies that are able to identify their Hedgehog Concept, and focus all of their efforts on that area, are more likely to achieve sustained success.

A Culture of Discipline

Chapter 6 emphasises the importance of maintaining a culture of discipline, in which everyone in the company is committed to achieving the company's goals, and holding themselves and each other accountable for their actions. The book argues that successful companies are those that are able to maintain a high level of discipline, and focus all of their efforts on achieving their goals.

Technology Accelerators

Chapter 7 focuses on the importance of embracing technology, and using it as a tool to improve productivity, streamline operations, and enhance the customer experience. The book argues that companies that are able to harness the power of technology are those that are best positioned for long-term success.

Conclusion

In conclusion, "Good to Great" by Jim Collins is a must-read for any business owner or entrepreneur who is looking to achieve sustained success. By emphasising the importance of building a strong foundation, hiring the right people, confronting the brutal facts, maintaining a culture of discipline, and embracing technology, the book provides a roadmap for achieving long-term success in any industry. As business owners, implementing the insights and action steps from this book can help us to achieve greater productivity, profitability, and success in our own companies.

"The 7 Habits of Highly Effective People" by Stephen Covey

This classic self-help book teaches readers how to improve their personal and professional effectiveness.

"The 7 Habits of Highly Effective People" by Stephen Covey provides a practical framework for achieving success in both personal and professional life through developing effective habits and adopting a proactive approach.

As a business owner, I'm constantly looking for ways to improve my effectiveness and achieve greater success. Stephen Covey's "The 7 Habits of Highly Effective People" is a timeless book that has provided practical guidance to millions of people around the world.

The book is based on the premise that success is the result of developing effective habits and adopting a proactive approach to life. Covey outlines a framework of seven habits that are essential to achieving success, both in personal and professional life.

Philosophy of the 7 Habits

The philosophy of the 7 Habits is based on the principle that individuals can take control of their lives and achieve success through adopting a proactive approach. Covey argues that individuals have the power to choose their responses to any situation and that this power is the key to achieving success.

The 7 Habits framework is designed to help individuals develop the habits and skills they need to achieve their goals, both in personal and professional life.

Key Takeaways

There are several key takeaways from the 7 Habits that can be applied to both personal and professional life:

1. Be proactive: Take responsibility for your own life and focus on the things that you can control.

2. Begin with the end in mind: Set clear goals and develop a plan to achieve them.

3. Put first things first: Prioritise your time and focus on the most important tasks.

4. Think win-win: Look for mutually beneficial solutions that create value for everyone.

5. Seek first to understand, then to be understood: Listen to others and seek to understand their perspectives before sharing your own.

6. Synergize: Work collaboratively with others to achieve common goals.

7. Sharpen the saw: Continuously improve your skills and knowledge in order to achieve greater effectiveness.

Action Steps

Here are some action steps that business owners can take to implement the 7 Habits:

1. Define your mission and goals: Begin with the end in mind by defining your mission and goals for your business. Develop a clear plan for achieving these goals.

2. Prioritise your time: Use Covey's time management matrix to prioritise your time and focus on the most important tasks.

3. Focus on win-win solutions: When negotiating with clients or partners, seek to create value for both parties by looking for win-win solutions.

4. Listen actively: Practise active listening when communicating with employees, partners, and customers. Seek to understand their perspectives before sharing your own.

5. Collaborate with others: Look for opportunities to collaborate with other businesses or entrepreneurs in order to achieve common goals.

6. Continuously improve: Make a commitment to continuously improve your skills and knowledge through ongoing education and training.

7. Live your values: Align your actions with your values and principles in order to achieve greater success and fulfilment.

Conclusion

"The 7 Habits of Highly Effective People" is a timeless book that provides practical guidance for achieving success in both personal and professional life. By adopting the 7 Habits framework, business owners can take control of their lives and achieve greater effectiveness in all areas of their business. The key takeaways of being proactive, setting clear goals, prioritising time, seeking win-win solutions, practising active listening, collaborating with others, and continuous improvement can be applied to any business, regardless of size or industry.

"The E-Myth Revisited" by Michael Gerber

This book explains how to create a successful business by focusing on systems and processes, rather than just the product or service.

"The E-Myth Revisited" by Michael E. Gerber teaches entrepreneurs how to build and grow their business by focusing on systems and processes, rather than on individual skills and talents.

As a business owner, I'm always looking for ways to improve my operations and grow my business. "The E-Myth Revisited" by Michael E. Gerber is a practical guide that has helped countless entrepreneurs to build and grow their businesses.

The book is based on the premise that most small businesses fail because their owners are too focused on working in the business, rather than on the business. Gerber argues that entrepreneurs need to adopt a more systematic approach to building and growing their businesses, which involves creating processes and systems that can be replicated and scaled.

Philosophy of the E-Myth

The E-Myth philosophy is based on the idea that most entrepreneurs start their businesses because they are skilled in a particular area or have a passion for a particular product or service. However, being skilled in a particular area does not necessarily translate into being a successful business owner.

Gerber argues that entrepreneurs need to focus on three distinct roles in their businesses: the technician, the manager, and the entrepreneur. The technician is the person who performs the technical work of the business, the manager is the person who manages the systems and processes, and the entrepreneur is the person who creates the vision and drives the growth of the business.

Key Takeaways

There are several key takeaways from the E-Myth that business owners can use to build and grow their businesses:

1. Create systems and processes: Develop systems and processes for every aspect of your business, from sales and marketing to operations and customer service.

2. Focus on working on the business, not in the business: Set aside time to work on the business, rather than just in the business. This involves developing a strategic plan for growth and focusing on creating systems and processes that can be replicated and scaled.

3. Embrace the role of the manager: The role of the manager is to

create and manage the systems and processes that drive the business. As an entrepreneur, it is important to recognize the value of this role and to delegate tasks to managers as necessary.

4. Create a franchise prototype: Develop a model for your business that can be replicated and scaled, as if you were creating a franchise. This involves developing processes and systems that can be easily taught and replicated by others.

5. Focus on delivering a consistent customer experience: Develop a system for delivering a consistent customer experience, from the initial contact to the final sale and beyond. This will help to build a strong reputation and create loyal customers.

Action Steps

Here are some action steps that business owners can take to implement the E-Myth philosophy:

1. Document your processes: Document every process and system in your business, from sales and marketing to operations and customer service. This will help to create consistency and ensure that everyone in the business is following the same procedures.

2. Create a strategic plan: Develop a strategic plan for growth that outlines your vision for the business and the steps you need to take to achieve it. This plan should focus on creating systems and processes that can be replicated and scaled.

3. Delegate tasks to managers: As an entrepreneur, it is important to delegate tasks to managers and other employees who can manage the systems and processes of the business.

4. Develop a franchise prototype: Develop a model for your business that can be replicated and scaled, as if you were creating a franchise. This involves developing processes and systems that can be easily taught and replicated by others.

5. Focus on the customer experience: Develop a system for delivering a consistent customer

Conclusion

In conclusion, "The E-Myth Revisited" by Michael Gerber is a transformative book that challenges the conventional view of entrepreneurship and provides a roadmap for building a successful business. By emphasising the importance of creating a system for managing every aspect of your business, Gerber shows us how to overcome the common pitfalls that often lead to failure. As business owners, implementing the insights and action steps from this book can help us to develop a clear vision, build a strong foundation, and create a culture of innovation and excellence. "The E-Myth Revisited" is a must-read for anyone looking to start a new business or improve an existing one, as it provides practical guidance on how to build a scalable and sustainable enterprise that can thrive in the long-term.

"The Innovator's Dilemma" by Clayton Christensen

This book explores the challenges that established companies face when trying to innovate, and offers insights on how to overcome them.

"The Innovator's Dilemma" by Clayton Christensen explores how successful companies can fail to innovate and adapt to disruptive technologies, and provides a framework for overcoming the innovator's dilemma.

As a business owner, you might be looking for ways to innovate and stay ahead of the competition. "The Innovator's Dilemma" by Clayton Christensen is a thought-provoking book that has helped me to understand the challenges of innovation in today's fast-changing market.

The book is based on the premise that successful companies can become trapped by their own success, and fail to innovate and adapt to disruptive technologies.

Christensen argues that companies need to adopt a more strategic approach to innovation, which involves investing in new technologies and markets, even if they seem less profitable in the short term.

Philosophy of the Innovator's Dilemma

The philosophy of the Innovator's Dilemma is based on the idea that successful companies can become too focused on their current products and customers, and fail to innovate and adapt to disruptive technologies. Christensen argues that companies need to be willing to invest in new technologies and markets, even if they seem less profitable in the short term.

The book introduces the concept of disruptive innovation, which is a type of innovation that creates a new market and value network, eventually disrupting an existing market and value network. Christensen argues that companies need to be willing to invest in disruptive technologies, even if they seem less profitable in the short term, in order to avoid being disrupted by competitors.

Key Takeaways

There are several key takeaways from the Innovator's Dilemma that business owners can use to innovate and stay ahead of the competition:

1. Invest in disruptive technologies: Invest in disruptive technologies and markets, even if they seem less profitable in the short term. This will help to create a new market and value network, and avoid being disrupted by competitors.

2. Focus on the job to be done: Focus on the customer's job to be done, rather than on the product or technology. By understanding the customer's needs and preferences, companies can create more innovative and effective products.

3. Create a culture of experimentation: Create a culture of experimentation and continuous learning, in order to stay ahead of the competition and adapt to changing market conditions.

4. Embrace the power of modularity: Embrace the power of modularity in product design, in order to create more flexible and adaptable products that can be easily upgraded and modified.

5. Create a separate business unit for disruptive innovation: Create a separate business unit or division for disruptive innovation, in order to allow for more experimentation and risk-taking, without disrupting the core business.

Action Steps

Here are some action steps that business owners can take to implement the Innovator's Dilemma philosophy:

1. Identify disruptive technologies and markets: Identify emerging technologies and markets that have the potential to disrupt your industry, and invest in them, even if they seem less profitable in the short term.

2. Focus on the customer's job to be done: Use customer research and feedback to understand the job to be done, and develop products and services that meet those needs.

3. Encourage experimentation and continuous learning: Create a culture of experimentation and continuous learning within the organisation, in order to stay ahead of the competition and adapt to changing market conditions.

4. Embrace the power of modularity: Design products with modularity in mind, in order to create more flexible and adaptable products that can be easily upgraded and modified.

5. Create a separate business unit for disruptive innovation: Create a separate business unit or division for disruptive innovation, in order to allow for more experimentation and risk-taking, without disrupting the core business

Conclusion

In conclusion, "The Innovator's Dilemma" by Clayton Christensen is a groundbreaking book that challenges the traditional notion of how businesses can sustain long-term success. By demonstrating how disruptive technologies can displace established businesses, Christensen shows us how to become more innovative and adaptive in a rapidly changing marketplace. As business owners, implementing the insights and action steps from this book can help us to identify potential disruptions, create a culture of innovation, and take calculated risks to stay ahead of the competition. "The Innovator's Dilemma" is an invaluable resource for anyone looking to become a more effective and innovative leader in their business, and to successfully navigate the challenges and opportunities of a constantly evolving marketplace.

"The One Minute Manager" by Kenneth Blanchard and Spencer Johnson

This book provides practical advice on how to become an effective manager and leader.

"The One Minute Manager" by Kenneth Blanchard and Spencer Johnson provides a simple yet powerful management philosophy that involves setting clear goals, providing effective feedback, and using positive reinforcement to achieve success.

"The One Minute Manager" by Kenneth Blanchard and Spencer Johnson

As a business owner, I'm always looking for ways to improve my management skills and motivate my employees. "The One Minute Manager" by Kenneth Blanchard and Spencer Johnson is a classic book that has provided practical guidance to millions of managers and leaders around the world.

The book is based on the premise that effective management involves setting clear goals, providing effective feedback, and using positive reinforcement to achieve success. The authors present a simple yet powerful management philosophy that can be applied to any industry or organisation.

Philosophy of the One Minute Manager

The philosophy of the One Minute Manager is based on three key principles: setting clear goals, providing effective feedback, and using positive reinforcement. The authors argue that these principles are essential for achieving success in any organisation or industry.

The One Minute Manager is described as someone who can manage themselves and others in a minute or less, and can be summarised as follows:

1. One Minute Goal Setting: The first step is to set clear goals that are concise, specific, and measurable. This involves agreeing on what needs to be accomplished and when it needs to be accomplished.

2. One Minute Praising: The second step is to provide effective feedback and positive reinforcement. This involves catching people doing things right and praising them for it.

3. One Minute Reprimand: The third step is to provide effective feedback when things are not going well. This involves providing feedback that is specific, timely, and focused on the behaviour, not the person.

Key Takeaways

There are several key takeaways from the One Minute Manager that business owners can use to improve their management skills and motivate their employees:

1. Set clear goals: Set clear goals that are concise, specific, and measurable. This will help to align everyone in the organisation and create a sense of focus and purpose.

2. Provide effective feedback: Provide effective feedback that is specific, timely, and focused on the behaviour, not the person. This will help to motivate employees and improve their performance.

3. Use positive reinforcement: Use positive reinforcement to motivate employees and create a positive work environment. This involves catching people doing things right and praising them for it.

4. Be a good listener: Listen to your employees and take their feedback seriously. This will help to create a sense of trust and respect in the organisation.

5. Keep it simple: Keep your management style simple and focused on the essentials. This will help to create clarity and avoid confusion.

Action Steps

Here are some action steps that business owners can take to implement the One Minute Manager philosophy:

1. Set clear goals: Set clear goals for yourself and your employees, and make sure that they are concise, specific, and measurable. This will help to align everyone in the organisation and create a sense of focus and purpose.

2. Provide effective feedback: Provide effective feedback that is specific, timely, and focused on the behaviour, not the person. This will help to motivate employees and improve their performance.

3. Use positive reinforcement: Use positive reinforcement to motivate employees and create a positive work environment. This involves catching people doing things right and praising them for it.

4. Be a good listener: Listen to your employees and take their feedback seriously. This will help to create a sense of trust and respect in the organisation.

5. Keep it simple: Keep your management style simple and focused on the essentials. This will help to create clarity and avoid confusion.

Conclusion

In conclusion, "The One Minute Manager" by Kenneth Blanchard and Spencer Johnson is a concise and practical guide to effective management that can help business owners to achieve greater productivity and results. By offering practical advice on how to set clear goals, provide immediate feedback, and recognize the contributions of your team, Blanchard and Johnson show us how to become more effective managers and leaders.

As business owners, implementing the insights and action steps from this book can help us to build a more motivated and productive team, achieve our business goals, and foster a positive work environment. "The One Minute Manager" is a valuable resource for anyone looking to become a more effective leader and achieve greater success in their business.

"Thinking, Fast and Slow" by Daniel Kahneman

This book provides insights into how the human mind works, and how we can make better decisions by understanding our cognitive biases.

"Thinking, Fast and Slow" by Daniel Kahneman explores the two systems of thought that govern our decision making processes, and provides practical insights into how we can make better decisions.

As the creative director and owner of a business I'm constantly making decisions that affect the success of my business. "Thinking, Fast and Slow" by Daniel Kahneman is a fascinating book that has helped me to better understand the way I think and make decisions.

The book is based on the premise that our decision-making processes are governed by two distinct systems of thought: System 1 (fast and intuitive) and System 2 (slow and deliberate). Kahneman argues that these systems of thought are prone to biases and errors, and provides practical insights into how we can make better decisions.

Philosophy of Thinking, Fast and Slow

The philosophy of "Thinking, Fast and Slow" is based on the idea that our minds operate in two different modes of thought: fast, intuitive, and automatic (System 1), and slow, deliberate, and effortful (System 2).

Kahneman argues that these two systems of thought work together in our minds, and that they are prone to biases and errors. He provides a wealth of examples and research to illustrate the ways in which these biases and errors can lead us astray.

The key to making better decisions, according to Kahneman, is to understand the ways in which our minds work, and to develop strategies for overcoming our biases and errors.

Key Takeaways

There are several key takeaways from "Thinking, Fast and Slow" that business owners can use to make better decisions:

1. Be aware of your biases: Recognize that your decision-making processes are prone to biases and errors, and actively work to overcome them.

2. Use System 2 thinking: Recognize the importance of slow, deliberate, and effortful thinking (System 2), and use it to make

important decisions.

3. Consider the base rate: Consider the base rate (the probability of an event occurring in a general population) when making decisions, rather than relying solely on personal experience.

4. Use a pre-mortem analysis: Use a pre-mortem analysis (imagining that a decision has already been made and then working backwards to identify potential problems) to identify potential problems before they arise.

5. Be willing to change your mind: Be willing to change your mind when presented with new evidence, and be open to the possibility that your initial assumptions may be incorrect.

Action Steps

Here are some action steps that business owners can take to implement the insights from "Thinking, Fast and Slow":

1. Develop a decision-making process: Develop a decision-making process that involves both fast, intuitive thinking (System 1) and slow, deliberate thinking (System 2).

2. Be aware of your biases: Be aware of your biases and actively work to overcome them. This can involve seeking out diverse perspectives, challenging your assumptions, and seeking out information that contradicts your beliefs.

3. Consider the base rate: Consider the base rate when making decisions, rather than relying solely on personal experience. This can involve gathering data and seeking out expert opinions.

4. Use a pre-mortem analysis: Use a pre-mortem analysis to identify potential problems before they arise. This can involve gathering a team of experts to analyse a decision and identify potential problems.

5. Be willing to change your mind: Be willing to change your mind when presented with new evidence, and be open to the possibility that your initial assumptions may be incorrect. This can involve seeking out information that contradicts your beliefs and being willing to adjust your plans accordingly.

Conclusion

In conclusion, "Thinking, Fast and Slow" is a thought-provoking and insightful book that provides practical guidance for improving decision-making processes. As a business owner, understanding the two systems of thought and how they interact with each other can help in making better decisions for the success of the business.

By implementing the suggested action steps, business owners can increase their awareness of biases and avoid errors, leading to more informed and effective decision-making processes. The book offers a wealth of examples and research to illustrate the ways in which biases can lead to incorrect decisions. By using both System 1 and System 2 thinking, considering the base rate, using pre-mortem analysis, and being willing to change our minds, we can make better decisions for our businesses.

"How to Win Friends and Influence People" by Dale Carnegie

This classic book offers timeless advice on how to build strong relationships and communicate effectively.

"How to Win Friends and Influence People" by Dale Carnegie is a timeless classic that teaches us how to build strong relationships and communicate effectively in both personal and professional settings.

As a business owner, I understand the importance of building strong relationships and communicating effectively with my employees and customers. "How to Win Friends and Influence People" by Dale Carnegie is a classic book that has helped millions of people improve their interpersonal skills and achieve success in both their personal and professional lives.

The book is based on the premise that people can be motivated and influenced by understanding their needs and desires, and by treating them with respect and consideration. Carnegie provides a wealth of practical advice and real-life examples to illustrate the power of effective communication and relationship building.

Philosophy of How to Win Friends and Influence People

The philosophy of "How to Win Friends and Influence People" is based on the idea that building strong relationships and effective communication are key to achieving success in both personal and professional settings.

Carnegie argued that by understanding the needs and desires of others, and by treating them with respect and consideration, we can build strong relationships that will help us achieve our goals. He provides a wealth of examples and advice on how to communicate effectively and build strong relationships, and stresses the importance of empathy and understanding.

Key Takeaways

There are several key takeaways from "How to Win Friends and Influence People" that business owners can use to build strong relationships and communicate effectively:

1. Show genuine interest in others: Show genuine interest in others by asking questions and listening attentively. This will help to build trust and rapport, and create a sense of mutual understanding.

2. Be a good listener: Be a good listener by focusing on what the other person is saying and demonstrating empathy. This will help to build trust and understanding, and create a sense of connection.

3. Give sincere compliments: Give sincere compliments and positive feedback to others. This will help to boost their self-esteem and create a positive and supportive work environment.

4. Use the power of influence: Use the power of influence by understanding the needs and desires of others, and by framing your message in a way that will resonate with them.

5. Be respectful and considerate: Be respectful and considerate towards others by treating them with dignity and respect, even in difficult or challenging situations.

Action Steps

Here are some action steps that business owners can take to implement the insights from "How to Win Friends and Influence People":

1. Show genuine interest in others: Show genuine interest in your employees and customers by asking questions and listening attentively. This will help to build trust and rapport, and create a sense of mutual understanding.

2. Be a good listener: Be a good listener by focusing on what the other person is saying and demonstrating empathy. This will help to build trust and understanding, and create a sense of connection.

3. Give sincere compliments: Give sincere compliments and

positive feedback to your employees and customers. This will help to boost their self-esteem and create a positive and supportive work environment.

4. Use the power of influence: Use the power of influence by understanding the needs and desires of your employees and customers, and by framing your message in a way that will resonate with them.

5. Be respectful and considerate: Be respectful and considerate towards your employees and customers by treating them with dignity and respect, even in difficult or challenging situations.

Conclusion

In conclusion, "How to Win Friends and Influence People" by Dale Carnegie is a timeless classic that provides practical guidance on how to build strong relationships and become a more effective communicator. By emphasising the importance of listening to others, showing genuine interest and appreciation, and understanding their point of view, Carnegie shows us how to create lasting connections and influence others in a positive way.

As business owners, implementing the insights and action steps from this book can help us to improve our communication skills, build strong relationships, and achieve greater success in our personal and professional lives. "How to Win Friends and

Influence People" is a must-read for anyone looking to become a more effective communicator and build strong, lasting relationships.

"The Art of War" by Sun Tzu

This ancient Chinese military treatise offers valuable lessons on strategy, leadership, and competition.

"The Art of War" by Sun Tzu is a classic book on military strategy that offers practical insights into leadership, decision-making, and conflict resolution.

As a business owner, I'm constantly making strategic decisions and facing conflicts that can impact the success of my business. "The Art of War" by Sun Tzu is a classic book on military strategy that has been applied to a wide range of fields, including business, politics, and sports.

The book is based on the premise that success in any endeavour requires careful planning, strategic thinking, and effective leadership. Sun Tzu offers practical insights into the art of war, including the importance of knowing oneself and one's enemy, understanding the terrain and environment, and using deception and strategic positioning.

Philosophy of The Art of War

The philosophy of "The Art of War" is based on the idea that success in any endeavour requires careful planning, strategic thinking, and effective leadership. Sun Tzu argues that effective leadership is essential for achieving success, and that leaders must understand their own strengths and weaknesses, as well as those of their enemies.

The book offers practical insights into the art of war, including the importance of understanding the terrain and environment, using deception and strategic positioning, and knowing when to attack and when to retreat. Sun Tzu stresses the importance of flexibility and adaptability, and encourages leaders to be creative and innovative in their approach to problem-solving.

Key Takeaways

There are several key takeaways from "The Art of War" that business owners can use to improve their leadership and decision-making:

1. Know thyself and thy enemy: Understand your own strengths and weaknesses, as well as those of your competitors, and use this knowledge to gain a strategic advantage.

2. Choose your battles wisely: Avoid unnecessary conflicts and focus your efforts on achieving your goals.

3. Use deception and strategic positioning: Use deception and strategic positioning to gain a strategic advantage over your competitors.

4. Be flexible and adaptable: Be flexible and adaptable in your approach to problem-solving, and be willing to change your tactics as the situation evolves.

5. Lead by example: Lead by example and inspire your team to achieve greatness.

Action Steps

Here are some action steps that business owners can take to implement the insights from "The Art of War":

1. Develop a strategic plan: Develop a strategic plan that takes into account your strengths and weaknesses, as well as those of your competitors.

2. Avoid unnecessary conflicts: Avoid unnecessary conflicts and focus your efforts on achieving your goals.

3. Use deception and strategic positioning: Use deception and strategic positioning to gain a strategic advantage over your competitors.

4. Be flexible and adaptable: Be flexible and adaptable in your approach to problem-solving, and be willing to change your tactics as the situation evolves.

5. Lead by example: Lead by example and inspire your team to achieve greatness by setting a high standard of behaviour and

work ethic.

Conclusion

"The Art of War" is a classic book that offers practical insights into leadership, decision-making, and conflict resolution. As a business owner, understanding the importance of strategic thinking, effective leadership, and adaptability can help to improve your decision-making and achieve success. By implementing the suggested action steps, business owners can apply the principles of "The Art of War" to their own business strategy and leadership style.

The book offers a wealth of practical advice and real-life examples to illustrate the power of effective leadership and strategic thinking.

"The Power of Now" by Eckhart Tolle

This book teaches readers how to live in the present moment and find inner peace, which can be useful for managing stress and improving focus in a business context.

"The Power of Now" by Eckhart Tolle is a transformative book that teaches us to live in the present moment, letting go of our past and future worries, and finding inner peace and joy.

As a business owner, I often find myself worrying about the future and dwelling on the past, which can lead to stress and anxiety. "The Power of Now" by Eckhart Tolle is a transformative book that offers practical guidance on how to live in the present moment, letting go of our past and future worries, and finding inner peace and joy.

The book is based on the premise that our thoughts and emotions are the root cause of our suffering, and that by learning to quiet our minds and focus on the present moment, we can free ourselves from the grip of negative thoughts and emotions. Tolle offers practical advice on how to achieve this state of presence, including meditation, mindfulness, and conscious breathing.

Philosophy of The Power of Now

The philosophy of "The Power of Now" is based on the idea that our thoughts and emotions are the root cause of our suffering, and that by learning to quiet our minds and focus on the present moment, we can free ourselves from the grip of negative thoughts and emotions. Tolle argues that the present moment is the only time that truly exists, and that by living in the present, we can find inner peace and joy.

The book offers practical insights into the nature of consciousness, the role of the ego, and the power of awareness. Tolle stresses the importance of cultivating a sense of presence and mindfulness in our daily lives, and encourages readers to let go of their attachment to material possessions and external circumstances.

Key Takeaways

There are several key takeaways from "The Power of Now" that business owners can use to improve their wellbeing and productivity:

1. Live in the present moment: Let go of your past and future worries, and focus on the present moment.

2. Quiet your mind: Practice meditation, mindfulness, and conscious breathing to quiet your mind and achieve a state of presence.

3. Let go of attachment: Let go of your attachment to material possessions and external circumstances, and focus on what truly matters in life.

4. Cultivate a sense of awareness: Cultivate a sense of awareness and mindfulness in your daily life, and observe your thoughts and emotions without judgement.

5. Embrace change: Embrace change and uncertainty as opportunities for growth and learning.

Action Steps

Here are some action steps that business owners can take to implement the insights from "The Power of Now":

1. Practice mindfulness: Practice mindfulness by taking a few moments each day to quiet your mind and focus on your breath.

2. Observe your thoughts and emotions: Observe your thoughts and emotions without judgement, and learn to let go of negative thoughts and emotions.

3. Let go of attachment: Let go of your attachment to material possessions and external circumstances, and focus on what truly matters in life.

4. Embrace change: Embrace change and uncertainty as opportunities for growth and learning, and stay open to new ideas

and perspectives.

5. Cultivate gratitude: Cultivate gratitude by taking time each day to reflect on the things in your life that you are thankful for.

Conclusion

In conclusion, "The Power of Now" by Eckhart Tolle is a transformative book that teaches us the value of living in the present moment, letting go of our past and future worries, and finding inner peace and joy. The book offers practical guidance on how to quiet our minds and focus on the present moment, and it emphasises the importance of cultivating a sense of awareness and mindfulness in our daily lives.

As business owners, we can apply the insights and action steps from this book to improve our wellbeing and productivity by practising mindfulness, letting go of attachment, and embracing change. "The Power of Now" is a powerful reminder that true success and happiness come from living in the present moment and cultivating a sense of inner peace and joy.

"Getting Things Done" by David Allen

This book provides practical advice on how to be more productive and organised, which can be especially useful for entrepreneurs and busy professionals.

"Getting Things Done" by David Allen is a practical guide to increase productivity, reduce stress, and achieve greater peace of mind through effective time management and organisation.

As a business owner, I am constantly juggling multiple tasks, projects, and deadlines, which can lead to stress and overwhelm. "Getting Things Done" by David Allen is a practical guide to increasing productivity, reducing stress, and achieving greater peace of mind through effective time management and organisation.

The book is based on the premise that our brains are not designed to hold and manage complex information, and that we need an external system to help us organise our thoughts and actions. Allen offers practical advice on how to create a system for managing tasks and projects, and he emphasises the importance of breaking down complex tasks into manageable steps.

Philosophy of Getting Things Done

The philosophy of "Getting Things Done" is based on the idea that effective time management and organisation are essential for reducing stress, increasing productivity, and achieving greater peace of mind. Allen argues that our brains are not designed to hold and manage complex information, and that we need an external system to help us organise our thoughts and actions.

The book offers practical insights into the nature of productivity, the importance of breaking down complex tasks into manageable steps, and the benefits of creating a system for managing tasks and projects. Allen stresses the importance of focusing on the most important tasks, and he encourages readers to create a clear vision of what they want to achieve.

Key Takeaways

There are several key takeaways from "Getting Things Done" that business owners can use to improve their productivity and reduce stress:

1. Create a system for managing tasks and projects: Create a system for managing tasks and projects, and use it consistently to stay organised and on track.

2. Break down complex tasks into manageable steps: Break down complex tasks into manageable steps to make them easier to manage and complete.

3. Focus on the most important tasks: Focus on the most important tasks that will have the greatest impact on achieving your goals.

4. Create a clear vision of what you want to achieve: Create a clear vision of what you want to achieve, and use it to guide your daily actions and decisions.

5. Use external tools to help you stay organised: Use external tools, such as a planner or task management software, to help you stay organised and manage your time effectively.

Action Steps

Here are some action steps that business owners can take to implement the insights from "Getting Things Done":

Create a task management system

Create a task management system, such as a to-do list or task management software, and use it consistently to stay organised and on track.

Break down complex tasks

Break down complex tasks into manageable steps, and schedule time in your calendar to complete each step.

Prioritise tasks

Prioritise tasks based on their importance and urgency, and focus on the most important tasks first.

Create a vision

Create a clear vision of what you want to achieve, and use it to guide your daily actions and decisions.

Use external tools

Use external tools, such as a planner or task management software, to help you stay organised and manage your time effectively.

Conclusion

In conclusion, "Getting Things Done" by David Allen is a practical guide to increase productivity, reduce stress, and achieve greater peace of mind through effective time management and organisation. By providing practical advice on creating a system for managing tasks and projects, breaking down complex tasks into manageable steps, and prioritising tasks based on their importance, Allen shows us how to become more organised and efficient. As business owners, implementing the insights and action steps from this book can help us to improve our productivity and reduce stress, enabling us to focus on the most important tasks that will have the greatest impact on achieving our goals.

"Getting Things Done" is a valuable resource for anyone looking to increase their productivity and manage their time more effectively.

"Built to Last" by Jim Collins and Jerry Porras

This book explores what sets the most enduring and successful companies apart from others, and offers insights on how to build a company that can stand the test of time.

"Built to Last" by Jim Collins is a classic business book that offers insights into what separates the most successful companies from the rest. The book is based on a six-year research project that analysed the performance of companies over a period of 50 years, comparing those that were able to achieve sustained success with those that did not. The study aimed to identify the key factors that led to long-term success, and the insights it offers have become essential reading for business owners, entrepreneurs, and leaders.

Philosophy of "Built to Last":

The philosophy of "Built to Last" is based on the idea that truly great companies are those that are able to achieve sustained success over the long-term, rather than just short-term gains. The book argues that this can only be achieved by building a strong foundation, developing a clear vision, and creating a culture of excellence. The most successful companies are those that are able to adapt to changes in the market and the economy, while remaining true to their core values and purpose.

Key Takeaways:

There are several key takeaways from "Built to Last" that business owners can use to improve their company's performance and achieve long-term success:

1. Build a strong foundation: Building a strong foundation is essential for achieving long-term success. This means developing a clear vision, establishing a culture of excellence, and creating a system for managing every aspect of the business.

2. Focus on core values: Successful companies are those that are able to identify and articulate their core values, and integrate them into every aspect of the business. This means creating a culture that is aligned with those values, and making sure that everyone in the company is committed to upholding them.

3. Set big, audacious goals: The most successful companies are those that are able to set big, audacious goals that inspire and motivate their teams. This means having a clear vision of where the company is going, and being willing to take risks to achieve that vision.

4. Embrace change: Companies that are able to adapt to changes in the market and the economy are those that are best positioned for long-term success. This means being willing to embrace new technologies, business models, and ways of doing things.

5. Hire the right people: In order to achieve sustained success,

companies need to have the right people in the right positions. This means hiring employees who are passionate, driven, and committed to achieving the company's goals.

Action Steps:

Here are some action steps that business owners can take to implement the insights from "Built to Last" in their own companies:

1. Develop a clear vision for your company, establish a culture of excellence, and create a system for managing every aspect of the business.

2. Identify your core values, and integrate them into every aspect of the business. Make sure that everyone in the company is committed to upholding those values.

3. Set big, audacious goals that inspire and motivate your teams. Have a clear vision of where the company is going, and be willing to take risks to achieve that vision.

4. Embrace change, and be willing to adapt to changes in the market and the economy. Keep an eye on new technologies, business models, and ways of doing things.

5. Hire employees who are passionate, driven, and committed to achieving the company's goals. Make sure that everyone in the company is aligned with the company's core values and vision.

Conclusion

In conclusion, "Built to Last" by Jim Collins is a must-read for any business owner or entrepreneur who is looking to achieve sustained success. By emphasising the importance of building a strong foundation, developing a clear vision, creating a culture of excellence, setting big, audacious goals, embracing change, and balancing competing objectives, the book provides a roadmap for achieving long-term success in any industry.

As business owners, implementing the insights and action steps from this book can help us to achieve greater productivity, profitability, and success in our own companies. "Built to Last" is a classic business book that provides practical guidance on how to build a scalable and sustainable enterprise that can thrive in the long-term.

"The Hard Thing About Hard Things" by Ben Horowitz

This book offers candid and practical advice on how to navigate the challenges of running a startup, including dealing with failure, making tough decisions, and managing teams.

"The Hard Thing About Hard Things" by Ben Horowitz is a book that provides insights into the challenges that business owners and entrepreneurs face when trying to build and grow a successful company. The book draws on Horowitz's personal experiences as a tech entrepreneur and venture capitalist, and offers practical guidance on how to navigate the many obstacles that come with running a business.

The book is a must-read for any business owner or entrepreneur who is looking to overcome the many challenges that come with starting and growing a company.

Philosophy of "The Hard Thing About Hard Things":

The philosophy of "The Hard Thing About Hard Things" is based on the idea that building and growing a successful company is a difficult and often painful process. The book emphasises the importance of being able to make tough decisions, manage through crises, and adapt to changes in the market and the economy. It also emphasises the importance of building a strong culture and team, and developing a clear strategy for achieving the company's goals.

Key Takeaways:

There are several key takeaways from "The Hard Thing About Hard Things" that business owners can use to improve their company's performance and achieve long-term success:

1. Embrace the struggle: Building and growing a successful company is a difficult and often painful process, but it is also incredibly rewarding. Business owners should be prepared to embrace the struggle, and view it as an opportunity to learn and grow.

2. Be a good leader: The most successful companies are those that are led by strong, effective leaders who are able to make tough decisions, manage through crises, and inspire their teams.

3. Build a strong culture and team: Creating a strong culture and team is essential for achieving long-term success. This means hiring the right people, developing a clear strategy, and fostering a culture of excellence.

4. Be adaptable: Companies that are able to adapt to changes in the market and the economy are those that are best positioned for long-term success. This means being willing to embrace new

technologies, business models, and ways of doing things.

5. Focus on the customer: Successful companies are those that are able to create products and services that meet the needs of their customers. This means focusing on the customer, and making sure that the company's products and services are designed to meet their needs.

Action Steps:

Here are some action steps that business owners can take to implement the insights from "The Hard Thing About Hard Things" in their own companies:

1. Embrace the struggle, and view it as an opportunity to learn and grow. Be prepared to make tough decisions, manage through crises, and adapt to changes in the market and the economy.

2. Be a good leader, and focus on developing the skills and qualities that are necessary for effective leadership. Make tough decisions, inspire your teams, and lead by example.

3. Build a strong culture and team by hiring the right people, developing a clear strategy, and fostering a culture of excellence. Make sure that everyone in the company is aligned with the company's goals and values.

4. Be adaptable, and keep an eye on new technologies, business models, and ways of doing things. Stay ahead of the curve, and be

willing to take calculated risks to stay ahead of the competition.

5. Focus on the customer, and make sure that the company's products and services are designed to meet their needs. Use customer feedback to guide product development and improve the customer experience.

Conclusion

In conclusion, "The Hard Thing About Hard Things" by Ben Horowitz is a must-read for any business owner or entrepreneur who is looking to build and grow a successful company. By emphasising the importance of being able to make tough decisions, manage through crises, adapt to changes in the market and the economy, and build a strong culture and team, the book provides practical guidance on how to overcome the many challenges that come with running a business.

As business owners, implementing the insights and action steps from this book can help us to achieve greater productivity, profitability, and success in our own companies. "The Hard Thing About Hard Things" is a powerful and inspiring book that offers a roadmap for achieving success in the face of adversity.

"Start With Why" by Simon Sinek

This book emphasises the importance of understanding your company's purpose and values, and how to use them to inspire and motivate employees and customers.

"Start With Why" by Simon Sinek is a book that explores the power of purpose in business and in life. The book argues that the most successful companies are those that start with a clear sense of purpose and vision, and that communicate that purpose and vision to their employees and customers. By focusing on the "why" of their business, rather than just the "what" or the "how," companies can inspire and motivate their employees, build a loyal customer base, and achieve long-term success.

Philosophy of "Start With Why"

The philosophy of "Start With Why" is based on the idea that purpose and meaning are the key drivers of success in business and in life. The book argues that the most successful companies are those that have a clear sense of purpose and vision, and that are able to communicate that purpose and vision to their employees and customers. By doing so, they are able to inspire and motivate their employees, build a loyal customer base, and achieve long-term success.

Key Takeaways:

There are several key takeaways from "Start With Why" that business owners can use to improve their company's performance and achieve long-term success:

1. Start with why: Successful companies are those that are able to articulate their purpose and vision in a clear and compelling way. By starting with "why," they are able to inspire and motivate their employees, build a loyal customer base, and achieve long-term success.

2. Build a culture of trust: Trust is essential for creating a culture of excellence and achieving long-term success. This means creating a work environment that values transparency, honesty, and open communication.

3. Hire the right people: Hiring the right people is essential for achieving long-term success. This means looking for people who share the company's values and vision, and who are committed to achieving the company's goals.

4. Communicate effectively: Effective communication is essential for building a strong culture, inspiring employees, and building a loyal customer base. This means communicating the company's purpose and vision in a clear and compelling way, and engaging in open and honest dialogue with employees and customers.

5. Focus on the long-term: Successful companies are those that are

able to focus on the long-term, and that are willing to invest in the future of the company. This means being willing to take calculated risks, and making decisions based on the company's long-term goals and vision.

Action Steps:

Here are some action steps that business owners can take to implement the insights from "Start With Why" in their own companies:

1. Start with why: Develop a clear sense of purpose and vision for your company, and communicate that purpose and vision to your employees and customers.

2. Build a culture of trust: Create a work environment that values transparency, honesty, and open communication. Encourage employees to share their ideas and opinions, and to engage in open and honest dialogue.

3. Hire the right people: Look for people who share the company's values and vision, and who are committed to achieving the company's goals. Focus on hiring for culture fit, as well as for skills and experience.

4. Communicate effectively: Communicate the company's purpose

and vision in a clear and compelling way, and engage in open and honest dialogue with employees and customers. Use storytelling to connect with your audience, and to inspire and motivate your employees.

5. Focus on the long-term: Make decisions based on the company's long-term goals and vision, and be willing to take calculated risks to achieve those goals. Avoid short-term thinking, and focus on building a sustainable business that can achieve long-term success.

Conclusion

In conclusion, "Start With Why" by Simon Sinek is a powerful and inspiring book that provides practical guidance on how to build a successful business. By starting with a clear sense of purpose and vision, and by communicating that purpose and vision in a compelling way, companies can inspire and motivate their employees, build a loyal customer base, and achieve long-term success.

As business owners, implementing the insights and action steps from this book can help us to achieve greater productivity, profitability, and success in our own companies. "Start With Why" is a must-read for any business owner or entrepreneur who is looking to build a purpose-driven company that can achieve long-term success.

"The 4-Hour Work Week" by Timothy Ferriss

This book provides a radical approach to time management and productivity, including strategies for outsourcing, automation, and working remotely.

The 4-Hour Work Week" by Timothy Ferriss is a book that challenges the traditional view of work and life, and offers a new perspective on how to achieve greater productivity, profitability, and fulfilment. The book argues that it is possible to live a life of leisure and adventure, while still achieving significant success in business and in life.

Philosophy of "The 4-Hour Work Week":

The philosophy of "The 4-Hour Work Week" is based on the idea of "lifestyle design," which is the process of designing your life and your work around your passions and your values. The book argues that it is possible to achieve greater productivity and profitability by working less, and by focusing on the 20% of activities that generate 80% of your results.

Key Takeaways:

There are several key takeaways from "The 4-Hour Work Week" that business owners can use to improve their productivity, profitability, and overall quality of life:

1. Focus on the 20%: The book argues that most of the work that we do is unnecessary, and that we can achieve greater productivity and profitability by focusing on the 20% of activities that generate 80% of our results.

2. Eliminate distractions: The book emphasises the importance of eliminating distractions, such as email and social media, in order to focus on the most important work.

3. Automate your business: The book argues that it is possible to automate many of the tasks that we do in our business, and that this can free up time and resources to focus on more important activities.

4. Outsource non-essential tasks: The book encourages business owners to outsource non-essential tasks, such as administrative work, in order to free up time and resources to focus on more important activities.

5. Take mini-retirements: The book argues that it is possible to achieve greater fulfilment and adventure by taking "mini-retirements" throughout your life, rather than waiting until retirement age.

Action Steps:

Here are some action steps that business owners can take to implement the insights from "The 4-Hour Work Week" in their own companies:

1. Focus on the 20%: Identify the 20% of activities that generate 80% of your results, and focus on those activities.

2. Eliminate distractions: Identify the distractions in your work environment, such as email and social media, and eliminate or minimise them as much as possible.

3. Automate your business: Look for opportunities to automate tasks in your business, such as customer service and marketing, in order to free up time and resources.

4. Outsource non-essential tasks: Identify the non-essential tasks in your business, such as administrative work, and outsource them to a virtual assistant or a third-party provider.

5. Take mini-retirements: Look for opportunities to take "mini-retirements" throughout your life, such as extended vacations or sabbaticals, in order to achieve greater fulfilment and adventure.

Conclusion

In conclusion, "The 4-Hour Work Week" by Timothy Ferriss is a powerful and inspiring book that provides practical guidance on how to achieve greater productivity, profitability, and fulfilment. By focusing on lifestyle design, eliminating distractions and non-essential tasks, automating our business, outsourcing tasks, and taking mini-retirements, we can achieve greater freedom and flexibility, while still achieving significant success in business and in life. As business owners, implementing the insights and action steps from this book can help us to achieve greater productivity, profitability, and success in our own companies.

"The 4-Hour Work Week" is a must-read for any business owner who wants to challenge the traditional view of work and life, and who wants to achieve greater freedom and flexibility in their business and in their life.

"The Outsiders" by William N. Thorndike

This book profiles eight highly successful CEOs who achieved outstanding results by thinking outside the box and bucking conventional wisdom.

"The Outsiders" by William N. Thorndike is a book that explores the leadership and management strategies of eight successful CEOs who are considered outsiders in their industries. The book provides valuable insights into the decision-making processes and strategies of these leaders, and offers actionable advice for business owners who want to emulate their success.

In the introduction of the book, the author provides an overview of the eight successful CEOs who are the focus of the book. He explains that these CEOs are considered outsiders because they operated in industries where they had little or no experience, and they did not conform to the conventional management strategies of their peers. The author also explains that the success of these CEOs can be attributed to their unconventional approaches to management and their focus on creating long-term value for their shareholders.

Chapter 1: "Teledyne's Henry Singleton"

Chapter 1 focuses on the leadership and management strategies of Henry Singleton, the CEO of Teledyne. The author explains that

Singleton was known for his unconventional approach to management, and his focus on creating long-term value for shareholders. The author also explains that Singleton was a master at capital allocation, and was able to generate significant returns for his shareholders by investing in businesses with high returns on capital.

Chapter 2: "Capital Cities' Tom Murphy"

Chapter 2 focuses on the leadership and management strategies of Tom Murphy, the CEO of Capital Cities. The author explains that Murphy was able to build Capital Cities into a successful media conglomerate by focusing on acquiring undervalued assets and integrating them into the company's existing operations. The author also explains that Murphy was a master at creating a culture of ownership and accountability within the company.

Chapter 3: "Kearney's Bill Anders"

Chapter 3 focuses on the leadership and management strategies of Bill Anders, the CEO of Kearney. The author explains that Anders was able to turn Kearney into a successful consulting firm by focusing on creating value for clients, and by investing in the development of the company's employees. The author also explains that Anders was a master at building relationships with clients and was able to generate significant business through word of mouth.

Chapter 4: "The Washington Post's Katharine Graham"

Chapter 4 focuses on the leadership and management strategies of Katharine Graham, the CEO of The Washington Post. The author explains that Graham was able to build The Washington Post into a successful media company by focusing on the quality of the company's journalism and by developing a strong corporate culture. The author also explains that Graham was a master at managing crises, and was able to navigate the Watergate scandal with integrity and professionalism.

Chapter 5: "General Dynamics' David Lewis"

Chapter 5 focuses on the leadership and management strategies of David Lewis, the CEO of General Dynamics. The author explains that Lewis was able to turn General Dynamics into a successful defence contractor by focusing on cost control and operational efficiency. The author also explains that Lewis was a master at capital allocation, and was able to generate significant returns for shareholders through share buybacks and dividend payments.

Chapter 6: "Rational's John Malone"

Chapter 6 focuses on the leadership and management strategies of John Malone, the CEO of Rational. The author explains that Malone was able to build Rational into a successful cable television company by focusing on creating value for customers and by investing in the development of new technologies. The author also explains that Malone was a master at negotiating and was able to acquire a significant amount of cable television assets through strategic deals.

Chapter 7: "T-Corp's Dick Smith"

Chapter 7 focuses on the leadership and management strategies of Dick Smith, the CEO of T-Corp. The author explains that Smith was able to turn T-Corp into a successful conglomerate by focusing on creating long-term value for shareholders and by investing in businesses that were undervalued. The author also explains that Smith was a master at cost control and was able to generate significant returns for shareholders by reducing the company's operating expenses.

Chapter 8: "Crosby's Chuck Knight"

Chapter 8 focuses on the leadership and management strategies of Chuck Knight, the CEO of Crosby. The author explains that Knight was able to turn Crosby into a successful manufacturing company by focusing on operational efficiency and by investing in the development of new technologies. The author also explains that Knight was a master at managing crises and was able to navigate a major labour strike with skill and professionalism.

Chapter 9: "The Outsiders' Commonalities"

Chapter 9 summarises the key takeaways from the book and identifies the commonalities between the successful CEOs who are the focus of the book. The author explains that the CEOs were able to achieve success by focusing on creating long-term value for shareholders, by investing in businesses with high returns on capital, and by building strong corporate cultures. The author also explains that the CEOs were able to achieve success by taking risks and by being willing to make tough decisions.

Action Steps for Business Owners:

After reading "The Outsiders," business owners can take several actionable steps to implement the strategies and approaches of the successful CEOs who are the focus of the book. Some of these steps include:

1. Focus on creating long-term value for shareholders: Business owners should focus on creating value for their shareholders over the long term, rather than chasing short-term profits.

2. Invest in businesses with high returns on capital: Business owners should invest in businesses with high returns on capital, rather than investing in businesses with low returns on capital.

3. Build strong corporate cultures: Business owners should focus on building strong corporate cultures that emphasise ownership

and accountability.

4. Take risks: Business owners should be willing to take risks and make tough decisions in order to achieve long-term success.

5. Emphasise operational efficiency: Business owners should focus on operational efficiency and cost control in order to generate significant returns for shareholders.

Conclusion

"The Outsiders" by William N. Thorndike is a valuable resource for business owners who are seeking new perspectives on leadership and management. The book provides insights into the decision-making processes and strategies of successful CEOs who are considered outsiders in their industries. By implementing the actionable advice provided in the book, business owners can improve their decision-making skills and achieve greater success over the long term.

"The Innovator's Solution" by Clayton Christensen and Michael Raynor

This book is a follow-up to "The Innovator's Dilemma," and provides practical guidance on how to create successful new products and services.

Most of us understand the importance of innovation and the need to constantly evolve and adapt to stay competitive. In "The Innovator's Solution," Clayton Christensen and Michael Raynor provide a comprehensive guide to innovation and offer practical advice for businesses looking to stay ahead of the curve.

Philosophy

At the heart of "The Innovator's Solution" is the philosophy that businesses must constantly innovate in order to stay ahead of the competition. Christensen and Raynor argue that many businesses fail to innovate because they focus too much on their existing products and customers, rather than looking for new growth opportunities.

To succeed in today's fast-paced business environment, the authors believe that businesses must adopt a "disruptive" approach to innovation. This means looking for new markets, developing new products and services, and challenging the status quo.

Key Takeaways

Disruptive Innovation

The most important takeaway from "The Innovator's Solution" is the concept of disruptive innovation. The authors argue that disruptive innovation is the key to success in today's business world, as it allows businesses to create new markets and outcompete established players.

Disruptive innovation involves identifying and targeting new or underserved markets with innovative products and services. The authors emphasise the importance of focusing on customer needs and creating solutions that are simpler, cheaper, and more accessible than existing products.

Action Step

Identify an underserved market or customer segment that could benefit from your products or services. Develop a solution that is tailored to their needs and is simpler, cheaper, or more accessible than existing offerings.

Focus on Jobs to Be Done

Another key takeaway from "The Innovator's Solution" is the

importance of focusing on "jobs to be done" when developing new products and services. The authors argue that customers don't buy products or services for their features or benefits, but rather to solve a specific problem or meet a specific need.

By focusing on the "job to be done," businesses can create solutions that are tailored to the customer's specific needs, rather than simply trying to improve on existing products or services.

Action Step

Conduct customer research to identify the jobs that your customers are trying to do with your products or services. Develop solutions that are specifically tailored to those needs.

Embrace Constraints

Christensen and Raynor argue that constraints can actually be a source of innovation and competitive advantage. Rather than trying to compete on features or benefits, businesses should focus on developing solutions that work within the constraints of the market or industry.

The authors provide several examples of successful companies that have embraced constraints, such as IKEA and Southwest Airlines. By focusing on simplicity and cost-effectiveness, these companies were able to disrupt their respective industries and gain a competitive advantage.

Action Step
Identify the constraints that exist within your market or industry. Develop solutions that work within those constraints, rather than trying to compete on features or benefits.

Develop a Capabilities System
Finally, the authors argue that businesses must develop a capabilities system to support innovation and growth. This involves building a set of core competencies and resources that allow the business to develop and launch new products and services.

The capabilities system should be built around the specific needs of the business and the market it operates in. It should include a focus on innovation, customer needs, and the ability to rapidly develop and launch new products and services.

Action Step
Develop a capabilities system that is tailored to the specific needs of your business and the market you operate in. This may involve investing in new technology, building a culture of innovation, or developing new partnerships and collaborations.

Implementing the Key Takeaways

Embrace Disruptive Innovation

To embrace disruptive innovation, it's important to look for new markets and customer segments that are underserved by existing products and services. This might involve conducting market research, identifying unmet needs, and developing solutions that are tailored to those needs.

One way to get started is to create a cross-functional team that is focused on disruptive innovation. This team can be tasked with identifying new growth opportunities and developing solutions that challenge the status quo.

Focus on Jobs to Be Done

To focus on jobs to be done, it's important to understand the specific needs and goals of your customers. This might involve conducting customer interviews or surveys, observing customer behaviour, and analysing customer data.

Once you have a clear understanding of the jobs that your customers are trying to do, you can develop solutions that are tailored to those needs. This might involve simplifying your products or services, making them more affordable, or making them more accessible to a broader customer base.

Embrace Constraints

To embrace constraints, it's important to understand the specific limitations and challenges of your market or industry. This might involve conducting a competitive analysis, studying industry trends, and analysing customer behaviour.

Once you have a clear understanding of the constraints that exist, you can develop solutions that work within those constraints. This might involve simplifying your products or services, streamlining your operations, or developing new partnerships and collaborations.

Develop a Capabilities System

To develop a capabilities system, it's important to focus on the specific needs of your business and the market you operate in. This might involve investing in new technology, building a culture of innovation, or developing new partnerships and collaborations.

One way to get started is to conduct a capabilities assessment to identify the strengths and weaknesses of your business. This can help you identify areas where you need to invest in new capabilities or resources to support innovation and growth.

Conclusion

In "The Innovator's Solution," Christensen and Raynor provide a comprehensive guide to innovation and offer practical advice for businesses looking to stay ahead of the curve. By emphasising the importance of disruptive innovation, focusing on jobs to be done, embracing constraints, and developing a capabilities system, the authors provide a roadmap for businesses looking to innovate and grow.

While these concepts may seem daunting, there are practical steps that business owners can take to implement them. By taking a systematic approach to innovation, businesses can stay ahead of the competition and succeed in today's fast-paced business environment.

"Measure What Matters" by John Doerr

This book introduces the concept of OKRs (Objectives and Key Results) and explains how to use them to set goals and track progress in a business context.

I recently read "Measure What Matters" by John Doerr, a venture capitalist who has been behind the success of many Silicon Valley companies, including Google, Intel, and Amazon. In the book, Doerr advocates for a system of setting and tracking goals that he calls Objectives and Key Results (OKRs). OKRs are a way to measure progress and keep teams focused on the most important tasks.

Doerr's philosophy is based on the belief that setting and tracking goals is the most effective way to achieve success. He argues that companies that are successful are those that set ambitious goals and then work hard to achieve them. In the book, Doerr shares his experiences working with some of the world's most successful companies and outlines the process of setting and tracking goals that he has used to help these companies achieve their goals.

Key Takeaways

Here are some of the key takeaways from "Measure What Matters" that I found particularly insightful and useful.

OKRs are a powerful tool for setting and achieving goals.
Doerr's central thesis is that the most successful companies are
those that set ambitious goals and then work hard to achieve them.
To do this effectively, he recommends using OKRs, which are a
way to set and track goals. OKRs consist of an objective, which is
a broad goal, and key results, which are measurable outcomes that
show progress towards the objective.

Setting ambitious goals is essential.

Doerr believes that setting ambitious goals is essential to
achieving success. He argues that when companies set ambitious
goals, they are more likely to achieve them than when they set
modest goals. The reason for this is that ambitious goals inspire
people to work harder and think more creatively.

Transparency is critical.

Doerr emphasises the importance of transparency in the goal-
setting process. He argues that when goals are made public, it
helps to create accountability and motivate people to work harder
to achieve them. This is why he recommends that OKRs be visible
to everyone in the company.

OKRs should be set at every level of the organisation.

Doerr believes that OKRs should be set at every level of the
organisation, from the CEO to the individual employee. This is

because everyone in the organisation has a role to play in achieving the company's goals. When everyone is working towards the same objectives, the company is more likely to succeed.

Continuous improvement is crucial.

Doerr emphasises the importance of continuous improvement. He argues that setting and achieving goals is a never-ending process, and that companies should always be looking for ways to improve. This means that OKRs should be reviewed regularly and revised as necessary.

Action Steps

Here are some action steps that business owners can take to implement the OKR system in their organisations.

Start with a clear mission statement.

Before you can set objectives and key results, you need to have a clear mission statement. Your mission statement should describe what your company does and why it exists. This will provide a framework for setting your OKRs.

Set objectives.

Once you have a clear mission statement, you can start setting objectives. Objectives should be broad, ambitious goals that are aligned with your mission statement. When setting objectives, it's important to think big and to set goals that will inspire your team.

Identify key results.

Once you have set your objectives, you need to identify key results that will help you measure progress towards those objectives. Key results should be specific, measurable outcomes that show progress towards the objective. Each objective should have 2-5 key results.

Make your OKRs visible.

Transparency is key when it comes to OKRs. Make sure that your OKRs are visible to everyone in the organisation. This will create accountability and motivate people to work harder to achieve their goals.

Set OKRs at every level of the organisation.

It's important to set OKRs at every level of the organisation, from the CEO to the individual employee. This will help ensure that everyone is working towards the same objectives and will create a sense of alignment throughout the organisation.

Review and revise OKRs regularly.

OKRs should be reviewed regularly and revised as necessary. This will help ensure that you stay on track towards your objectives and that you are always looking for ways to improve.

Celebrate successes.

When you achieve your objectives, it's important to celebrate your successes. This will create a sense of accomplishment and motivate your team to continue working hard towards the next set of goals.

Learn from failures.

Not every objective will be achieved, and that's okay. It's important to learn from failures and use that knowledge to set better objectives in the future.

Conclusion

"Measure What Matters" is a valuable resource for any business owner looking to set and achieve ambitious goals. Doerr's OKR system provides a framework for setting objectives and key results that can help organisations stay focused and achieve success. By implementing the OKR system and following the action steps outlined in the book, business owners can create a culture of goal-setting and continuous improvement that can help them achieve their most important objectives.

"Leaders Eat Last" by Simon Sinek

This book explores the importance of creating a positive and supportive work culture, and how to lead with empathy and integrity.

In the book, Sinek argues that great leaders prioritise the needs of their team above their own needs. He suggests that leaders who are willing to put the well-being of their team first will inspire greater trust, loyalty, and performance from their team members.

Sinek's philosophy is based on the idea that leadership is about serving others, not about being served. In the book, he shares stories and research to support this idea and offers practical advice on how to become a leader who puts the needs of others first.

Key Takeaways

Here are some of the key takeaways from "Leaders Eat Last" that I found particularly insightful and useful.

Leaders who prioritise the needs of their team inspire greater trust and loyalty.

Sinek argues that when leaders prioritise the needs of their team members above their own needs, they inspire greater trust and loyalty from their team. This is because team members feel that their leader cares about them and is willing to do what it takes to support them.

Safety is a fundamental need.

Sinek emphasises the importance of creating a safe environment for team members. He argues that safety is a fundamental human need and that when people feel safe, they are more likely to be productive and creative.

Empathy is essential.

Sinek believes that empathy is essential to great leadership. He argues that leaders who are able to understand and relate to the emotions of their team members are more likely to create a sense of trust and loyalty.

Leadership is a choice.

Sinek emphasises that leadership is a choice, not a position. He argues that anyone can be a leader, regardless of their job title or position in the organisation. All it takes is a willingness to put the needs of others first.

Servant leadership is the most effective form of leadership.

Sinek advocates for a form of leadership called servant leadership, in which the leader prioritises the needs of their team members above their own needs. He believes that this is the most effective form of leadership because it creates a culture of trust, loyalty, and performance.

Action Steps

Here are some action steps that business owners can take to implement the principles of "Leaders Eat Last" in their organisations.

Prioritise safety.

To create a safe environment for your team members, start by establishing clear safety protocols and guidelines. This can include things like workplace safety procedures, anti-harassment policies, and mental health support resources. Make sure that everyone in the organisation is aware of these policies and understands their importance.

Practice empathy.

To become a more empathetic leader, start by listening more and talking less. When team members come to you with a problem, take the time to understand their perspective and validate their feelings. You can also practise empathy by putting yourself in your team members' shoes and trying to understand their experience.

Lead by example.

To inspire your team to prioritise the needs of others, lead by example. Take the time to listen to your team members, show them that you care about their well-being, and make decisions that are in their best interest. When you prioritise the needs of your team members, they are more likely to follow your example.

Encourage teamwork and collaboration.

To create a culture of trust and collaboration, encourage teamwork and collaboration in your organisation. This can include things like team-building activities, group projects, and opportunities for cross-functional collaboration. When team members work together towards a common goal, they are more likely to develop trust and loyalty towards one another.

Recognize and reward good behaviour.

To reinforce the importance of prioritising the needs of others, recognize and reward good behaviour. This can include things like acknowledging team members who have gone above and beyond to help their colleagues or celebrating team successes. When you recognize and reward good behaviour, you create a culture that values teamwork and collaboration.

Develop a sense of purpose.

To create a sense of purpose in your organisation, start by defining a clear mission and vision. Make sure that everyone in the organisation understands what the company stands for and what its goals are. When team members feel that they are working towards a meaningful goal, they are more likely to be motivated and engaged.

Invest in your team members.

To show your team members that you care about their well-being, invest in their professional development. This can include things like training programs, mentorship opportunities, and opportunities for career advancement. When you invest in your team members, you demonstrate that you are committed to their success.

Foster open communication.

To create a culture of trust and collaboration, it's important to foster open communication in your organisation. This can include things like regular team meetings, one-on-one meetings with team members, and opportunities for feedback and input. When team members feel that their voices are heard, they are more likely to feel valued and engaged.

Conclusion

"Leaders Eat Last" offers valuable insights into what it takes to be a great leader who prioritises the needs of their team members. By creating a safe environment, practising empathy, leading by example, encouraging teamwork and collaboration, recognizing and rewarding good behaviour, developing a sense of purpose, investing in team members, and fostering open communication, business owners can create a culture of trust, loyalty, and performance in their organisations. Sinek's philosophy of servant leadership offers a powerful framework for achieving success through prioritising the needs of others.

"Zero to One" by Peter Thiel

This book provides insights on how to create and capture new value in a rapidly changing world, and offers advice on how to build a successful startup from scratch.

"Zero to One" by Peter Thiel is a business book that provides insights on how to build a successful startup from scratch. Thiel is an entrepreneur, venture capitalist, and co-founder of PayPal, who has been involved in numerous successful startups. In "Zero to One," Thiel emphasises the importance of creating a unique and innovative product or service, and explains why copying or competing with existing businesses is not a recipe for success. The book is filled with valuable lessons and actionable steps that can help aspiring entrepreneurs and established businesses alike.

The Philosophy of Zero to One

The fundamental philosophy of "Zero to One" is that entrepreneurs should strive to create something new, rather than copying or improving upon existing products or services. Thiel argues that creating something new is the only way to build a successful and sustainable business. In his view, innovation is what drives progress and creates value, and without it, businesses will struggle to differentiate themselves from their competitors.

One of the key insights of the book is the importance of creating a monopoly. Thiel argues that a monopoly is the most effective way to build a sustainable and profitable business. A monopoly is defined as a company that is the only provider of a particular product or service. Thiel argues that monopolies are not only good for businesses, but they are also good for society. Monopolies allow companies to focus on long-term goals and invest in research and development, which ultimately benefits everyone.

Key Takeaways

Start with a Big Idea

According to Thiel, the most successful businesses start with a big idea that is different from anything that currently exists in the market. Rather than trying to improve upon existing products or services, entrepreneurs should focus on creating something entirely new.

Create a Monopoly

Thiel argues that creating a monopoly is the most effective way to build a sustainable and profitable business. By being the only provider of a particular product or service, companies can focus on long-term goals and invest in research and development.

Focus on Vertical Progression

Thiel distinguishes between horizontal and vertical progress. Horizontal progress is when companies improve upon existing products or services, while vertical progress is when they create something entirely new. Thiel argues that vertical progress is more important because it drives innovation and creates value.

Build a Strong Team

Thiel emphasises the importance of building a strong team. He believes that a company is only as good as its team, and that hiring the right people is critical to success.

Focus on Sales

Thiel believes that sales are the most important aspect of any business. He argues that without sales, a business is just an idea, and that entrepreneurs should focus on selling their product or service as early as possible.

Action Steps

Identify a Big Idea

To create something new, entrepreneurs need to start with a big idea. Identify a problem or need in the market that is not currently being addressed and develop a solution.

Research the Market

Before investing time and resources into a new business idea, it's important to research the market to ensure that there is a demand for the product or service.

Focus on Vertical Progress

Rather than trying to compete with existing businesses, focus on creating something entirely new. This will require a lot of creativity and innovation, but it's the only way to build a sustainable and profitable business.

Build a Strong Team

Building a strong team is critical to the success of any business. Identify the key roles that need to be filled and hire the best people for the job.

Focus on Sales

Sales are the lifeblood of any business. As soon as a product or service is developed, start focusing on sales. This will help validate the business idea and generate revenue.

Conclusion

"Zero to One" by Peter Thiel provides a unique perspective on what it takes to build a successful startup. Thiel's emphasis on creating something new and unique is an important reminder that competition is not the only path to success. The book challenges entrepreneurs to think outside the box and strive for vertical progression, rather than simply trying to improve upon existing products or services.

One of the key takeaways from "Zero to One" is the importance of building a strong team. Thiel believes that a company is only as good as its team, and that hiring the right people is critical to success. As a business owner, it's important to identify the key roles that need to be filled and hire the best people for the job. This requires a thorough understanding of the skills and expertise required for each role, as well as a commitment to finding the right people who can help take the business to the next level.

Thiel also emphasises the importance of sales, which he believes are the most important aspect of any business. Without sales, a business is just an idea. Entrepreneurs should focus on selling their product or service as early as possible to validate their business idea and generate revenue. This will require a lot of hard work and persistence, but it's the only way to build a successful business.

In conclusion, "Zero to One" is a must-read for anyone interested in starting a business or improving an existing one. Thiel provides valuable insights and actionable steps that can help entrepreneurs create something new and unique, build a strong team, and focus on sales. By following Thiel's advice, businesses can differentiate themselves from their competitors and build a sustainable and profitable business.

"The Fifth Discipline" by Peter Senge

This book introduces the concept of the "learning organisation," and provides insights on how to build a company that is capable of continuous learning and adaptation.

"The Fifth Discipline" by Peter Senge is a book that explores the principles and practices of what it takes to build a learning organisation. A learning organisation is one that is able to adapt and grow in response to changes in the environment, and one that fosters a culture of learning, collaboration, and innovation. The book provides a framework for building a learning organisation, and outlines the key disciplines that are necessary to create such an organisation.

The Philosophy of The Fifth Discipline

The fundamental philosophy of "The Fifth Discipline" is that organisations must become learning organisations in order to thrive in an increasingly complex and dynamic environment. According to Senge, learning organisations are those that have the ability to learn, adapt, and innovate at every level, from individual employees to the organisation as a whole. The five disciplines that are necessary to create a learning organisation are personal mastery, mental models, shared vision, team learning, and systems thinking.

Key Takeaways

Personal Mastery

Personal mastery is the discipline of continually clarifying and deepening our personal vision, of focusing our energies, of developing patience, and of seeing reality objectively. It is about learning to live our lives in the present moment, and constantly seeking to improve ourselves in all areas of life. Personal mastery requires a commitment to lifelong learning and personal growth.

Mental Models

Mental models are the assumptions and beliefs that we have about the world around us. They shape our perceptions, influence our behaviour, and affect the decisions that we make. In order to become a learning organisation, it is important to challenge and examine our mental models, and to be open to new and different ways of thinking.

Shared Vision

Shared vision is the process of developing a clear and compelling picture of the future that we want to create, and communicating that vision to everyone in the organisation. A shared vision provides a sense of purpose and direction, and helps to align everyone's efforts towards a common goal.

Team Learning

Team learning is the process of aligning the talents and energies of individuals towards a common goal. It is about creating an environment that encourages open communication, collaboration, and learning from one another. Team learning requires trust, respect, and a commitment to working together towards a shared vision.

Systems Thinking

Systems thinking is the discipline of seeing the interrelationships that are present in complex systems, and understanding how those interrelationships affect the behaviour of the system as a whole. It is about understanding the big picture, and recognizing that everything is connected. Systems thinking is a critical discipline for building a learning organisation, as it allows us to identify the underlying causes of problems and to create effective solutions.

Action Steps

Personal Mastery

To develop personal mastery, business owners should focus on creating a culture of lifelong learning and personal growth. This can be achieved by providing opportunities for employees to learn new skills, offering mentoring and coaching programs, and encouraging employees to pursue their passions.

Mental Models

To challenge and examine mental models, business owners should encourage open and honest communication in the organisation. This can be achieved by creating a culture of feedback, where employees are encouraged to share their thoughts and ideas, and to challenge the status quo. Business owners should also be open to new and different ways of thinking, and should seek out diverse perspectives and experiences.

Shared Vision

To develop a shared vision, business owners should involve employees in the visioning process, and ensure that everyone understands the purpose and direction of the organisation. This can be achieved by creating a culture of transparency and openness, and by regularly communicating the vision to everyone in the organisation. Business owners should also encourage employees to contribute to the vision, and to take ownership of the goals and objectives of the organisation.

Team Learning

To foster team learning, business owners should create an environment that encourages collaboration and open communication. This can be achieved by creating opportunities for employees to work together on projects, and by providing resources and tools that support collaboration. Business owners should also encourage employees to share their knowledge and expertise with one another, and to learn from one another's experiences.

Systems Thinking

To develop systems thinking, business owners should encourage employees to look at the big picture and to consider how their actions and decisions affect the organisation as a whole. This can be achieved by providing training and resources on systems thinking, and by creating a culture that values and rewards systems thinking. Business owners should also create opportunities for employees to collaborate across departments and functions, and to develop a deep understanding of the interrelationships between different parts of the organisation.

Conclusion

"The Fifth Discipline" by Peter Senge provides a powerful framework for building a learning organisation that can adapt and thrive in a complex and dynamic environment. The book emphasises the importance of personal mastery, mental models, shared vision, team learning, and systems thinking as the key disciplines that are necessary to create a learning organisation. Business owners who are committed to creating a learning organisation can use the insights and action steps provided in the book to foster a culture of lifelong learning, collaboration, and innovation.

By doing so, they can build an organisation that is able to adapt and grow in response to changes in the environment, and that is better positioned to achieve long-term success.

"Blue Ocean Strategy" by W. Chan Kim and Renee Mauborgne

This book offers a framework for creating new market opportunities and disrupting existing markets by focusing on innovation and value creation.

"Blue Ocean Strategy" by W. Chan Kim and Renee Mauborgne is a business book that provides a framework for creating new markets, rather than competing in existing ones. The authors argue that businesses should focus on creating "blue oceans" - untapped market spaces with high potential for growth and profitability - rather than fighting over the same customers in existing markets. The book provides insights on how to identify and develop blue oceans, and offers practical tools and frameworks to help businesses create and capture new market opportunities.

The Philosophy of Blue Ocean Strategy

The fundamental philosophy of "Blue Ocean Strategy" is that businesses can create new markets and unlock new growth opportunities by focusing on value innovation. Value innovation is the process of creating new and unique value for customers that is not currently offered in the market. By doing so, businesses can create new demand and establish themselves as market leaders in a blue ocean of untapped potential.

Key Takeaways

Red Ocean vs. Blue Ocean: Red oceans are existing markets where companies compete for the same customers, often resulting in a "bloody" battle for market share. Blue oceans, on the other hand, are untapped market spaces where businesses can create new demand and establish themselves as market leaders.

Value Innovation

Value innovation is the process of creating new and unique value for customers that is not currently offered in the market. By doing so, businesses can create new demand and establish themselves as market leaders in a blue ocean of untapped potential.

The Four Actions Framework

The Four Actions Framework provides a tool for identifying and developing blue oceans. It involves identifying the key factors that customers value in the industry, and then creating a new value curve that is different from that of existing competitors.

The Six Paths Framework

The Six Paths Framework provides a tool for identifying new market opportunities by looking across six different dimensions: customer, industry, strategic group, complementary product/service, functional/emotional appeal, and time.

Non-Customer Analysis

Non-customer analysis involves identifying potential customers who are not currently being served by the industry, and developing strategies to capture their business. This can be a powerful way to unlock new growth opportunities and create a blue ocean of untapped potential.

Action Steps

Identify Existing Market Space

To create a blue ocean strategy, business owners must first identify the existing market space in which their business operates. This involves identifying the key factors that customers value in the industry, and understanding how existing competitors are meeting those needs.

Create a Value Curve

Once the existing market space has been identified, business owners can use the Four Actions Framework to create a new value curve that is different from that of existing competitors. This involves identifying the key factors that customers value, and then identifying the actions that the business can take to create a new value curve.

Explore the Six Paths

The Six Paths Framework provides a tool for identifying new market opportunities by looking across six different dimensions. Business owners should explore each of these dimensions to identify potential blue ocean opportunities.

Non-Customer Analysis

Non-customer analysis involves identifying potential customers who are not currently being served by the industry, and developing strategies to capture their business. Business owners should explore this dimension to identify potential new market opportunities.

Focus on Value Innovation

Business owners should focus on value innovation, which involves creating new and unique value for customers that is not currently offered in the market. By doing so, businesses can create new demand and establish themselves as market leaders in a blue ocean of untapped potential.

Conclusion

"Blue Ocean Strategy" by W. Chan Kim and Renee Mauborgne is a powerful tool for businesses that are looking to unlock new growth opportunities and create a blue ocean of untapped potential. The book provides practical tools and frameworks that can be used by business owners to identify and develop blue oceans, and offers valuable insights on the importance of value innovation. By following the action steps outlined in the book, business owners can create a new value curve that is different from that of existing competitors, and explore new market opportunities across different dimensions.

One of the key takeaways from the book is the importance of non-customer analysis, which involves identifying potential customers who are not currently being served by the industry, and developing strategies to capture their business. This can be a powerful way to unlock new growth opportunities and create a blue ocean of untapped potential. Business owners should be open to exploring this dimension and identifying potential new market opportunities.

The Four Actions Framework is another valuable tool that can be used to identify and develop blue oceans. This involves identifying the key factors that customers value in the industry, and then creating a new value curve that is different from that of existing competitors. By doing so, businesses can create new demand and establish themselves as market leaders in a blue ocean of untapped potential.

In conclusion, "Blue Ocean Strategy" is a must-read for business owners who are looking to unlock new growth opportunities and create a blue ocean of untapped potential. The book provides a powerful framework for identifying and developing blue oceans, and offers practical tools and frameworks that can be used to create and capture new market opportunities. By following the action steps outlined in the book, business owners can create a new value curve that is different from that of existing competitors, and explore new market opportunities across different dimensions. By doing so, they can establish themselves as market leaders and unlock new growth opportunities in a competitive and dynamic environment.

"The Art of Possibility" by Rosamund Stone Zander and Benjamin Zander

This book offers a fresh perspective on leadership and creativity, and provides practical guidance on how to approach challenges with a positive and open mindset.

"The Art of Possibility" by Rosamund Stone Zander and Benjamin Zander is a book that challenges us to re-examine our beliefs and assumptions about what is possible in our personal and professional lives. The book provides a set of principles and practices that can help us shift our mindset from one of limitation to one of possibility, and create new opportunities for growth and development.

The Philosophy of The Art of Possibility

The fundamental philosophy of "The Art of Possibility" is that we can create new possibilities in our lives by changing the way we see and interpret the world around us. The book argues that we often limit ourselves by our beliefs and assumptions, and that by challenging these limitations, we can create new opportunities for growth and development.

Key Takeaways

Giving an A

Giving an A is the practice of seeing the potential in others, and treating them as if they have already achieved their full potential. This creates a sense of possibility and opens up new opportunities for growth and development.

Rule Number 6

Rule Number 6 is the practice of not taking ourselves too seriously, and of recognizing that we are not the centre of the universe. By letting go of our ego and our need for control, we can create a more relaxed and open environment that fosters creativity and innovation.

It's All Invented

It's All Invented is the practice of recognizing that the stories we tell ourselves about the world are just that - stories. By acknowledging that these stories are not necessarily true, we can open ourselves up to new possibilities and create new opportunities for growth and development.

Being a Contribution

Being a Contribution is the practice of focusing on what we can give to others, rather than what we can get from them. By being a contribution, we create a sense of abundance and possibility, and open ourselves up to new opportunities for growth and development.

Leading from Any Chair

Leading from Any Chair is the practice of recognizing that anyone can be a leader, regardless of their position or status. By leading from any chair, we create a sense of possibility and open ourselves up to new opportunities for growth and development.

Action Steps

Giving an A

To practise giving an A, business owners should focus on seeing the potential in others, and treating them as if they have already achieved their full potential. This can be achieved by providing opportunities for employees to grow and develop, and by recognizing and celebrating their achievements.

Rule Number 6

To practice Rule Number 6, business owners should focus on creating a relaxed and open environment that fosters creativity and innovation. This can be achieved by encouraging open communication, embracing failure as a learning opportunity, and creating a culture of experimentation.

It's All Invented

To practise It's All Invented, business owners should focus on challenging their own assumptions and beliefs, and being open to new possibilities. This can be achieved by creating opportunities for employees to share their thoughts and ideas, and by encouraging diverse perspectives and experiences.

Being a Contribution

To practise Being a Contribution, business owners should focus on what they can give to others, rather than what they can get from them. This can be achieved by creating a culture of collaboration, and by recognizing and celebrating the contributions of others.

Leading from Any Chair

To practise Leading from Any Chair, business owners should focus on creating a culture where everyone is encouraged to take ownership and responsibility for their work. This can be achieved by providing opportunities for employees to lead and take on new challenges, and by recognizing and celebrating their contributions.

Conclusion

"The Art of Possibility" by Rosamund Stone Zander and Benjamin Zander provides a powerful framework for shifting our mindset from one of limitation to one of possibility. The book offers a set of principles and practices that can help us create new opportunities for growth and development, and challenge our beliefs and assumptions about what is possible. By following the action steps outlined in the book, business owners can create a culture of possibility, collaboration, and innovation.

One of the key takeaways from the book is the importance of giving an A - seeing the potential in others, and treating them as if they have already achieved their full potential. This can be a powerful way to create a culture of possibility and open up new opportunities for growth and development. Business owners should be open to recognizing and celebrating the achievements of their employees, and providing opportunities for them to grow and develop.

Another important takeaway is the practice of being a contribution - focusing on what we can give to others, rather than what we can get from them. This can be achieved by creating a culture of collaboration and recognizing the contributions of others. By doing so, business owners can create a sense of abundance and possibility, and open themselves up to new opportunities for growth and development.

In conclusion, "The Art of Possibility" is a powerful tool for business owners who are looking to create a culture of possibility, collaboration, and innovation. The book provides a set of principles and practices that can help us shift our mindset from one of limitation to one of possibility, and create new opportunities for growth and development. By following the action steps outlined in the book, business owners can create a culture of possibility and openness, and unlock new opportunities for growth and success.

"The Culture Code" by Daniel Coyle

This book explores what makes great teams and organisations successful, and provides practical guidance on how to create a positive and high-performing work culture.

"The Culture Code" by Daniel Coyle is a book that explores the key elements of high-performing teams and organisations. The book provides insights and action steps that business owners can use to create a culture of excellence, collaboration, and innovation. By following the principles and practices outlined in the book, business owners can create a culture that fosters success and drives long-term growth.

The Philosophy of The Culture Code

The fundamental philosophy of "The Culture Code" is that the most successful teams and organisations have a strong culture that is built on three key elements: safety, vulnerability, and purpose. These elements create a sense of belonging and shared identity, and allow teams and organisations to work together to achieve common goals and objectives.

Key Takeaways

Safety

Safety is the foundation of a strong team culture. It involves creating an environment where team members feel safe to be themselves, to take risks, and to make mistakes. This can be achieved by creating a culture of respect, trust, and psychological safety.

Vulnerability

Vulnerability is the key to building strong relationships and creating a sense of belonging. It involves being open and honest with team members, and sharing our thoughts, feelings, and experiences. This can be achieved by creating opportunities for team members to connect on a personal level, and by encouraging open communication and feedback.

Purpose

Purpose is the driving force behind high-performing teams and organisations. It involves having a clear and compelling vision, and a shared sense of identity and mission. This can be achieved by creating a culture of shared values, and by setting clear and meaningful goals and objectives.

Action Steps

Create a Culture of Safety

To create a culture of safety, business owners should focus on creating an environment where team members feel safe to be themselves, to take risks, and to make mistakes. This can be achieved by creating a culture of respect, trust, and psychological safety. Business owners should encourage open communication and feedback, and provide opportunities for team members to share their thoughts and experiences.

Foster Vulnerability

To foster vulnerability, business owners should create opportunities for team members to connect on a personal level, and encourage open communication and feedback. This can be achieved by providing team-building activities, such as off-site retreats or team-building exercises, and by creating a culture of open communication and feedback.

Clarify Purpose

To clarify purpose, business owners should create a clear and compelling vision, and a shared sense of identity and mission. This can be achieved by setting clear and meaningful goals and objectives, and by creating a culture of shared values. Business owners should also communicate the vision and mission of the organisation regularly, and ensure that team members are aligned with these goals and objectives.

Lead by Example

To create a culture of excellence, collaboration, and innovation, business owners should lead by example. This involves embodying the values and behaviours that are essential to the culture of the organisation, and setting an example for team members to follow. Business owners should model the behaviours and attitudes that they want to see in their team members, and create a culture of accountability and continuous improvement.

Conclusion

"The Culture Code" by Daniel Coyle provides a powerful framework for creating a culture of excellence, collaboration, and innovation. The book emphasises the importance of safety, vulnerability, and purpose as the key elements of a strong team culture, and provides action steps that business owners can use to create a culture that fosters success and drives long-term growth.

By following the principles and practices outlined in the book, business owners can create a culture that allows team members to work together to achieve common goals and objectives, and drive long-term success for the organisation.

"Drive" by Daniel Pink

This book explains what motivates people, and provides insights on how to create a work environment that fosters intrinsic motivation and creativity.

"Drive" by Daniel Pink is a book that challenges traditional thinking about what motivates people in the workplace. The book provides a new perspective on motivation, arguing that people are driven by intrinsic motivators such as autonomy, mastery, and purpose. By understanding these motivators, business owners can create a more engaging and fulfilling work environment that fosters creativity, innovation, and productivity.

The Philosophy of Drive

The fundamental philosophy of "Drive" is that people are motivated by intrinsic factors such as autonomy, mastery, and purpose, rather than external factors such as rewards and punishment. The book argues that by providing employees with autonomy, opportunities for mastery, and a sense of purpose, business owners can create a more engaging and fulfilling work environment that fosters creativity, innovation, and productivity.

Key Takeaways
Autonomy

Autonomy is the ability to control one's own work and make decisions about how to accomplish goals. By providing employees with autonomy, business owners can create a more engaging work environment that fosters creativity, innovation, and productivity.

Mastery

Mastery is the desire to get better at something that matters. By providing employees with opportunities for mastery, business owners can create a culture of continuous improvement and innovation.

Purpose

Purpose is the sense that one's work has meaning and makes a difference in the world. By providing employees with a sense of purpose, business owners can create a more fulfilling work environment that fosters engagement and motivation.

Action Steps

Provide Autonomy

To provide employees with autonomy, business owners should focus on creating a culture of trust and empowerment. This can be achieved by giving employees control over their own work, setting clear expectations, and providing regular feedback and support.

Foster Mastery

To foster mastery, business owners should focus on creating opportunities for skill development and continuous improvement. This can be achieved by providing employees with training and development programs, challenging assignments, and opportunities to collaborate with others.

Create a Sense of Purpose

To create a sense of purpose, business owners should focus on creating a culture of shared values and a clear sense of mission. This can be achieved by communicating the organisation's mission and values regularly, and by providing opportunities for employees to connect their work to a larger purpose.

Create a Culture of Feedback

To create a culture of feedback, business owners should focus on creating a culture of continuous improvement and collaboration. This can be achieved by providing regular feedback and support, encouraging open communication and feedback, and recognizing and celebrating the contributions of team members.

Conclusion

"Drive" by Daniel Pink provides a new perspective on motivation, arguing that people are driven by intrinsic factors such as autonomy, mastery, and purpose. By understanding these motivators, business owners can create a more engaging and fulfilling work environment that fosters creativity, innovation, and productivity. By providing employees with autonomy, opportunities for mastery, and a sense of purpose, business owners can create a culture of continuous improvement and innovation that drives long-term growth and success for the organisation.

By following the action steps outlined in the book, business owners can create a culture of trust, empowerment, and collaboration that allows team members to work together to achieve common goals and objectives.

"The Goal" by Eliyahu Goldratt

This book is a novel that provides a practical guide to the Theory of Constraints, and offers insights on how to improve operational efficiency and profitability.

One of the most widely read business books of all time, "The Goal" by Eliyahu Goldratt is a novel that tells the story of a troubled manufacturing plant and the challenges its manager, Alex Rogo, faces to turn it around. Throughout the book, Goldratt presents his Theory of Constraints, which aims to help businesses identify and overcome bottlenecks in their processes. This chapter summary will explore the main philosophy, key takeaways, and actionable steps that business owners can take to implement the lessons of "The Goal."

Key Takeaways

1. A business's goal is to make money, not just to produce goods or services.

2. The Theory of Constraints (TOC) is a systematic approach to identifying and overcoming bottlenecks in a business's processes.

3. The three measures of flow: throughput, inventory, and operational expense, are used to evaluate a business's performance.

4.The five steps of the TOC process: identify the system's constraints, decide how to exploit the constraint, subordinate everything else to the above decisions, elevate the system's constraint, and repeat the process.

5. A balanced plant is not the same as a productive plant.

6. Organisations must constantly improve to stay competitive.

"The Goal" is a novel that tells the story of a manufacturing plant manager, Alex Rogo, who is facing a crisis. His plant is losing money, and he must find a way to turn it around before it's too late. Throughout the book, Goldratt presents his Theory of Constraints (TOC), which is a systematic approach to identifying and overcoming bottlenecks in a business's processes.

Action Steps to Implement

Identify bottlenecks: Take a closer look at your business processes to identify potential bottlenecks. Look for areas where work accumulates, where queues are forming, and where people are waiting for others to complete their tasks. Once you identify these bottlenecks, focus on finding ways to increase their throughput and reduce the time it takes for work to flow through these areas.

Measure performance

Develop metrics and KPIs to measure the performance of your

business processes. This will help you track your progress over time and identify areas that need improvement. Use these metrics to guide your decision-making process and to determine whether changes are having a positive impact on your business.

Focus on flow

Think about the flow of work through your organisation. Work to identify areas where work is flowing smoothly and efficiently and where there are blockages or constraints. Use this information to identify areas where you can optimise the flow of work and reduce the time it takes to complete tasks.

Continuously improve

Identify areas of your business that need improvement and work to continuously improve them. Use the insights you gain from measuring performance, identifying bottlenecks, and focusing on flow to identify areas where you can make changes that will have a positive impact on your business.

Encourage collaboration

Collaboration is key to improving business processes. Encourage your team members to work together to identify areas for improvement and to develop new solutions. This will help to ensure that everyone is working towards the same goals and will help to create a culture of continuous improvement.

Eliminate waste

Look for ways to eliminate waste in your business processes. This can include reducing the amount of inventory you carry, streamlining processes to reduce the time it takes to complete tasks, and reducing the number of steps required to complete a task. By eliminating waste, you can improve efficiency and reduce costs.

Focus on your customers

Finally, focus on your customers. Understand their needs and work to develop solutions that will meet those needs. This will help to ensure that you are delivering value to your customers and that they are satisfied with the products and services you provide.

Conclusion

"The Goal" by Eliyahu Goldratt is a classic business book that offers a fresh perspective on process improvement. By focusing on the flow of work through an organisation and identifying bottlenecks, businesses can make changes that will have a positive impact on efficiency and effectiveness. Through the use of the Theory of Constraints and the application of the five-step process of continuous improvement, businesses can work to optimise their processes and reduce waste. By encouraging collaboration and focusing on the needs of their customers, businesses can deliver value and achieve success.

"Competitive Strategy" by Michael Porter

This book is a classic in the field of strategy, and provides a framework for analysing competitive forces and developing a successful business strategy.

Competitive Strategy by Michael Porter is a seminal work in the field of business strategy. The book outlines a framework for analysing the competitive environment and developing a winning strategy. In this chapter summary, I will provide an overview of the book, highlight its main philosophy and key takeaways, and provide actionable steps that a business owner can take to implement these ideas.

Competitive Strategy was first published in 1980 and has since become a classic in the field of business strategy. The book is divided into three parts. Part One provides an introduction to the concept of competitive strategy and outlines the framework that Porter will use throughout the book. Part Two focuses on the two basic types of competitive advantage: cost leadership and differentiation. Part Three explores the strategies that companies can use to compete in different industries and situations.

Main Philosophy

At the heart of Porter's philosophy is the idea that a company can only achieve sustained competitive advantage by choosing a unique and sustainable position in its industry. This position is achieved through either cost leadership or differentiation. A company that is a cost leader produces goods or services at a lower cost than its competitors, while a company that differentiates itself provides goods or services that are perceived as unique or superior to those of its competitors. Porter argues that companies that pursue a middle-of-the-road strategy and attempt to be both cost leaders and differentiators will not achieve sustained competitive advantage.

Porter also emphasises the importance of understanding the five forces that shape the competitive environment: the threat of new entrants, the bargaining power of suppliers, the bargaining power of buyers, the threat of substitute products or services, and the intensity of competitive rivalry. By analysing these forces, companies can develop a better understanding of the competitive environment and develop strategies that take advantage of opportunities and neutralise threats.

Key Takeaways

1. Choose a unique and sustainable position in your industry: Companies that achieve sustained competitive advantage do so by

choosing a unique and sustainable position in their industry. This position is achieved through either cost leadership or differentiation. Companies that attempt to be both cost leaders and differentiators will not achieve sustained competitive advantage.

2. Understand the five forces that shape the competitive environment: The competitive environment is shaped by five forces: the threat of new entrants, the bargaining power of suppliers, the bargaining power of buyers, the threat of substitute products or services, and the intensity of competitive rivalry. By analysing these forces, companies can develop a better understanding of the competitive environment and develop strategies that take advantage of opportunities and neutralise threats.

3. Focus on creating value for customers: Companies that differentiate themselves do so by creating value for their customers. This value can be achieved through product quality, customer service, brand reputation, or other factors that are important to customers.

4. Continuously improve operational efficiency: Companies that are cost leaders achieve their position by continuously improving operational efficiency. This can be achieved through process improvement, supply chain optimization, or other methods that reduce costs while maintaining quality.

5. Develop a culture of innovation: Companies that achieve sustained competitive advantage are often characterised by a

culture of innovation. This can be achieved by encouraging employees to think creatively, rewarding new ideas, and fostering a culture of experimentation.

Action Steps for Business Owners

Analyse the competitive environment

Begin by analysing the five forces that shape the competitive environment: the threat of new entrants, the bargaining power of suppliers, the bargaining power of buyers, the threat of substitute products or services, and the intensity of competitive rivalry. Use this analysis to identify opportunities and threats in the competitive environment.

Choose a unique and sustainable position

Based on your analysis of the competitive environment, choose a unique and sustainable position in your industry. This position should be based on either cost leadership or differentiation. Avoid attempting to be both a cost leader and a differentiator.

Develop a value proposition

Once you have chosen your position, develop a clear and compelling value proposition that communicates the unique value that your company provides to customers. This value proposition should be based on the needs and wants of your target customers and should clearly differentiate your company from its competitors.

Continuously improve operational efficiency

If you have chosen to pursue a cost leadership strategy, focus on continuously improving operational efficiency. This can be achieved through process improvement, supply chain optimization, or other methods that reduce costs while maintaining quality. Regularly monitor your costs and look for ways to reduce them without sacrificing quality.

Focus on creating value for customers

If you have chosen to pursue a differentiation strategy, focus on creating value for your customers. This can be achieved through product quality, customer service, brand reputation, or other factors that are important to customers. Regularly solicit feedback from customers and use this feedback to improve your products or services.

Foster a culture of innovation

To achieve sustained competitive advantage, it is important to foster a culture of innovation within your company. Encourage employees to think creatively, reward new ideas, and foster a culture of experimentation. Regularly invest in research and development to stay ahead of the competition.

Monitor and adapt

Finally, it is important to regularly monitor the competitive environment and adapt your strategy as needed. Keep a close eye on the five forces that shape the competitive environment and look for changes that could impact your business. Be willing to pivot your strategy if needed to take advantage of new opportunities or neutralise threats.

Conclusion

Competitive Strategy by Michael Porter is a must-read for any business owner or manager who wants to develop a winning strategy. Porter's framework provides a clear and practical approach to analysing the competitive environment and developing a unique and sustainable position in your industry. By focusing on either cost leadership or differentiation, and by continuously improving operational efficiency and creating value for customers, businesses can achieve sustained competitive advantage and thrive in their industry. By fostering a culture of innovation and being willing to adapt to changes in the competitive environment, businesses can stay ahead of the competition and continue to grow and succeed over the long term.

"The Innovator's Mindset" by George Couros

This book encourages readers to develop a mindset of innovation, and provides practical guidance on how to foster creativity and innovation in a business context.

The Innovator's Mindset by George Couros is a book that explores the mindset of innovators and how they approach challenges and opportunities. The book outlines a framework for developing an innovator's mindset, and provides examples of how this mindset can lead to success in business, education, and other fields. In this chapter summary, I will provide an overview of the book, highlight its main philosophy and key takeaways, and provide actionable steps that a business owner can take to implement these ideas.

The Innovator's Mindset was first published in 2015 and has since become a popular resource for anyone looking to develop a more innovative approach to problem-solving. The book is divided into three parts. Part One provides an introduction to the concept of the innovator's mindset and outlines the framework that Couros will use throughout the book.

Part Two focuses on the eight characteristics of the innovator's mindset, which include being empathetic, being a risk-taker, and being a networker. Part Three explores how to put the innovator's mindset into practice, including ways to cultivate innovation in teams and organisations.

Main Philosophy

At the heart of Couros' philosophy is the idea that anyone can develop an innovator's mindset, regardless of their background or experience. The innovator's mindset is characterised by a willingness to take risks, a willingness to learn from failure, and a willingness to collaborate and network with others. Innovators are also empathetic and have a deep understanding of the needs and wants of their customers and users.

Couros argues that the innovator's mindset is not just a way of thinking, but also a way of being. It is a set of habits and behaviours that can be developed and strengthened over time. By cultivating an innovator's mindset, individuals and organisations can become more agile, more creative, and more successful.

Key Takeaways

1. Take risks: Innovators are willing to take risks and try new things. They are not afraid of failure, and they see failure as an opportunity to learn and grow.

2. Be empathetic: Innovators have a deep understanding of the needs and wants of their customers and users. They are empathetic and seek to create products and services that meet the needs of their customers.

3. Be a networker: Innovators collaborate and network with others to share ideas and resources. They understand that innovation often comes from unexpected sources, and they seek out diverse perspectives to fuel their creativity.

4. Embrace change: Innovators are comfortable with change and see it as an opportunity for growth and improvement. They are always looking for ways to improve their products and services and to stay ahead of the competition.

5. Be a lifelong learner: Innovators are always learning and seeking out new information and skills. They understand that the world is constantly changing, and they need to keep up in order to stay relevant and successful.

Action Steps for Business Owners

Encourage risk-taking: Create a culture that encourages risk-taking and experimentation. Encourage employees to try new things and to learn from failure. Provide support and resources for employees who are taking risks, and celebrate their successes and failures.

Foster empathy

Develop a deep understanding of the needs and wants of your customers and users. Encourage employees to spend time with customers and to listen to their feedback. Use this feedback to inform your product and service development process.

Encourage networking

Encourage employees to collaborate and network with others, both inside and outside of your organisation. Provide opportunities for employees to attend conferences and events, and to connect with others in their field. Encourage cross-functional teams and diverse perspectives.

Embrace change

Embrace change and be open to new ideas and approaches. Encourage employees to challenge the status quo and to think creatively. Foster a culture of continuous improvement and encourage employees to look for ways to improve your products and services.

Invest in learning

Provide opportunities for employees to learn and develop new skills. Invest in training and development programs, and encourage employees to pursue continuing education and professional development opportunities. Create a culture that values learning and rewards employees for their efforts to improve themselves and the organisation.

Develop a process for innovation

Create a process for innovation that encourages employees to generate and develop new ideas. Provide resources and support for employees who are working on new projects, and encourage cross-functional collaboration. Regularly review and assess your innovation process to ensure that it is working effectively.

Celebrate innovation

Celebrate innovation and recognize employees who are taking risks and trying new things. Publicly acknowledge their contributions and reward them for their successes. This will help to reinforce a culture of innovation and encourage others to take risks and try new things.

Conclusion

The Innovator's Mindset by George Couros provides a practical and actionable framework for developing an innovator's mindset. By encouraging risk-taking, fostering empathy, networking, embracing change, investing in learning, developing a process for innovation, and celebrating innovation, businesses can become more agile, creative, and successful. By cultivating an innovator's mindset, businesses can stay ahead of the competition, create new opportunities, and thrive in a constantly changing environment.

"Building a StoryBrand" by Donald Miller

This book provides a framework for creating a clear and compelling brand message, and offers practical guidance on how to communicate that message effectively.

Building a StoryBrand by Donald Miller is a book that provides a framework for developing a clear and compelling brand story. The book outlines a seven-part process for creating a brand story that engages customers and drives business success. In this chapter summary, I will provide an overview of the book, highlight its main philosophy and key takeaways, and provide actionable steps that a business owner can take to implement these ideas.

Overview of the Book

Building a StoryBrand was first published in 2017 and has since become a popular resource for anyone looking to develop a strong brand story. The book is divided into two parts. Part One provides an introduction to the concept of story and outlines the framework that Miller will use throughout the book. Part Two focuses on the seven-part framework for creating a clear and compelling brand story, which includes elements such as identifying a customer's problem, offering a solution, and providing a call to action.

Main Philosophy

At the heart of Miller's philosophy is the idea that businesses need to tell a clear and compelling story in order to connect with customers and drive business success. This story should be focused on the customer's needs and desires, and should offer a solution to their problems. Miller argues that businesses often make the mistake of focusing on themselves and their products or services, rather than on the customer's needs and desires.

Miller's seven-part framework for creating a clear and compelling brand story is designed to help businesses create a story that engages customers and drives business success. By focusing on the customer's needs and desires, and by offering a clear and compelling solution to their problems, businesses can connect with customers on an emotional level and build a strong brand.

Key Takeaways

1. Focus on the customer's needs and desires: The most effective brand stories focus on the customer's needs and desires, rather than on the business's products or services. By understanding the customer's problems and desires, businesses can create a story that engages them and drives business success.

2. Offer a clear and compelling solution: Businesses should offer a clear and compelling solution to the customer's problems. This

solution should be easy to understand and should offer clear benefits to the customer.

3. Keep the message simple: A simple message is more memorable and effective than a complicated one. Businesses should focus on a single, clear message that is easy to understand and remember.

4. Use a story structure: Stories are more engaging and memorable than facts and figures. Businesses should use a story structure to create a narrative that engages customers and drives business success.

5. Provide a clear call to action: A clear call to action is essential to driving business success. Businesses should provide a clear and compelling call to action that encourages customers to take action.

Action Steps for Business Owners

Identify your customer's problems and desires

Spend time understanding your customer's problems and desires. Conduct market research, talk to customers, and analyse data to gain a deep understanding of their needs and desires.

Offer a clear and compelling solution

Develop a clear and compelling solution to the customer's

problems. This solution should be easy to understand and should offer clear benefits to the customer. Develop messaging that clearly communicates the benefits of your solution.

Keep the message simple

Focus on a single, clear message that is easy to understand and remember. Use simple language and avoid jargon or technical terms that might confuse customers.

Use a story structure

Use a story structure to create a narrative that engages customers and drives business success. Develop a clear protagonist (the customer), a problem that needs to be solved, and a clear and compelling solution. Use storytelling elements like tension, conflict, and resolution to create a compelling narrative.

Provide a clear call to action

Provide a clear and compelling call to action that encourages customers to take action. Use language that is action-oriented and encourages customers to take the next step. Make it easy for customers to take action, whether that means clicking a button on your website, calling your business, or visiting your store.

Test and refine your message

Test your brand story with customers to see how they respond.

Use feedback to refine your message and make it more effective. Use data and analytics to track the effectiveness of your messaging and make adjustments as needed.

Consistently communicate your story

Consistently communicate your brand story across all channels, including your website, social media, advertising, and customer interactions. Make sure that your messaging is consistent and aligned with your brand story.

Measure the effectiveness of your message

Measure the effectiveness of your messaging and track how it is driving business success. Use data and analytics to identify areas where you can improve and make adjustments as needed.

Conclusion

Building a StoryBrand by Donald Miller provides a practical and actionable framework for developing a clear and compelling brand story. By focusing on the customer's needs and desires, offering a clear and compelling solution, keeping the message simple, using a story structure, providing a clear call to action, testing and refining your message, consistently communicating your story, and measuring the effectiveness of your message, businesses can create a brand story that engages customers and drives business success.

By telling a clear and compelling story that resonates with customers, businesses can build a strong brand and stand out in a crowded marketplace.

"Purple Cow: Transform Your Business by Being Remarkable" by Seth Godin

This book encourages businesses to stand out by being remarkable, and provides practical guidance on how to create products and marketing campaigns that are truly unique.

Purple Cow is a book that challenges businesses to be "remarkable" in order to stand out in a crowded marketplace. The book argues that businesses can no longer rely on traditional marketing and advertising strategies, and that they must be willing to take risks and be remarkable in order to succeed. In this chapter summary, I will provide an overview of the book, highlight its main philosophy and key takeaways, and provide actionable steps that a business owner can take to implement these ideas.

Overview of the Book

Purple Cow was first published in 2003 and has since become a popular resource for anyone looking to stand out in a crowded marketplace. The book is divided into three parts. Part One provides an introduction to the concept of the purple cow and why it is important for businesses to be remarkable. Part Two explores the practical aspects of creating a remarkable product or service, including developing a unique value proposition, creating a powerful brand, and generating word of mouth. Part Three explores how to put the purple cow philosophy into practice, including ways to integrate the philosophy into business culture and how to apply it to marketing and advertising strategies.

Main Philosophy

At the heart of Godin's philosophy is the idea that businesses must be "remarkable" in order to succeed in a crowded marketplace. Being "remarkable" means standing out from the competition and being memorable and distinctive. Godin argues that traditional marketing and advertising strategies are no longer effective, and that businesses must be willing to take risks and be remarkable in order to succeed.

The "purple cow" metaphor is used to illustrate this philosophy. A purple cow is a remarkable and distinctive sight, and is something that people will talk about and remember. Godin argues that businesses must be like purple cows in order to stand out in a crowded marketplace.

Key Takeaways

1. Be remarkable: To succeed in a crowded marketplace, businesses must be remarkable. This means standing out from the competition and being memorable and distinctive. Being "good enough" is not enough - businesses must be remarkable in order to

succeed.

2. Develop a unique value proposition: A unique value proposition is essential to creating a remarkable product or service. Businesses should focus on developing a clear and compelling value proposition that differentiates them from the competition.

3. Create a powerful brand: A powerful brand is essential to standing out in a crowded marketplace. Businesses should focus on developing a strong brand identity that is distinctive and memorable.

4. Generate word of mouth: Word of mouth is the most powerful form of marketing, and is essential to creating a remarkable product or service. Businesses should focus on creating a product or service that is so remarkable that people will talk about it and share it with others.

5. Take risks: Being remarkable requires taking risks. Businesses should be willing to take risks and try new things in order to stand out from the competition.

Action Steps for Business Owners

Develop a unique value proposition

Spend time developing a unique value proposition that differentiates your business from the competition. Identify what sets you apart from your competitors and focus on highlighting these differences in your messaging and marketing.

Create a powerful brand

Develop a strong brand identity that is distinctive and memorable. Invest in branding and design, and develop messaging that is consistent with your brand identity.

Focus on creating a remarkable product or service

Focus on creating a product or service that is so remarkable that people will talk about it and share it with others. This could be achieved through innovative design, exceptional customer service, or other factors that set your product or service apart from the competition.

Generate word of mouth

Encourage customers to share their experiences with your product or service on social media and other platforms. Provide incentives for customers who refer others to your business.

Take risks

Be willing to take risks and try new things in order to stand out from the competition. Experiment with new marketing and advertising strategies, and be willing to pivot when something is not working.

Foster a culture of innovation

Foster a culture of innovation within your business by encouraging employees to take risks and try new things. Reward employees who come up with innovative ideas and provide resources and support to help them bring their ideas to life.

Focus on customer experience

Focus on creating an exceptional customer experience that sets you apart from the competition. Pay attention to every touchpoint in the customer journey, from the first interaction with your brand to the final sale and beyond.

Continuously improve

Continuously improve your product or service in order to maintain your competitive edge. Regularly gather feedback from customers and use this feedback to make improvements and iterate on your product or service.

Be authentic

Be authentic and true to your brand identity. Don't try to be something that you're not, as customers will see through this and it will damage your credibility.

Conclusion

Purple Cow: Transform Your Business by Being Remarkable by Seth Godin provides a practical and actionable framework for developing a remarkable product or service. By developing a unique value proposition, creating a powerful brand, generating word of mouth, taking risks, fostering a culture of innovation, focusing on customer experience, continuously improving, and being authentic, businesses can stand out in a crowded marketplace and drive business success. By being willing to take risks and try new things, businesses can differentiate themselves from the competition and create a memorable and distinctive brand.

"Influence: The Psychology of Persuasion" by Robert Cialdini

This book explains the principles of persuasion and how they can be applied to marketing and advertising.

Influence: The Psychology of Persuasion by Robert Cialdini is a classic book that explores the psychology of persuasion and how businesses can use it to influence customers. The book outlines six principles of persuasion, including reciprocity, scarcity, authority, consistency, liking, and social proof. In this chapter summary, I will provide an overview of the book, highlight its main philosophy and key takeaways, and provide actionable steps that a business owner can take to implement these ideas.

Overview of the Book

Influence was first published in 1984 and has since become a classic resource for anyone looking to understand the psychology of persuasion. The book is divided into six chapters, each of which explores one of the six principles of persuasion. The principles are illustrated with real-world examples and practical advice for how businesses can use them to influence customers.

Main Philosophy

At the heart of Cialdini's philosophy is the idea that businesses can use the principles of persuasion to influence customers and drive business success. The six principles of persuasion are universal and can be applied in a wide range of contexts, from marketing and advertising to sales and negotiations.

Cialdini argues that businesses must understand the psychology of persuasion in order to influence customers effectively. By understanding the six principles of persuasion and how they work, businesses can develop more effective marketing and advertising strategies, close more sales, and negotiate more effectively.

Key Takeaways

1. Reciprocity: Reciprocity is the principle that people are more likely to give when they receive something first. Businesses can use reciprocity by offering something of value to customers, such as a free trial or a free sample, in order to encourage them to purchase their products or services.

2. Scarcity: Scarcity is the principle that people are more likely to want something that is scarce or in limited supply. Businesses can use scarcity by highlighting the limited availability of their products or services, or by creating a sense of urgency around purchasing.

3. Authority: Authority is the principle that people are more likely

to trust and follow the advice of someone who is perceived as an authority figure. Businesses can use authority by positioning themselves or their products as being endorsed by experts or by using testimonials from satisfied customers.

4. Consistency: Consistency is the principle that people are more likely to follow through on something if they have made a public commitment to it. Businesses can use consistency by asking customers to make a public commitment to their products or services, or by using small commitments to lead customers to larger commitments.

5. Liking: Liking is the principle that people are more likely to be influenced by people they like. Businesses can use liking by developing relationships with customers, being friendly and approachable, and highlighting similarities between themselves and their customers.

6. Social proof: Social proof is the principle that people are more likely to follow the actions of others. Businesses can use social proof by highlighting the popularity of their products or services, using customer reviews and testimonials, and creating a sense of community around their brand.

Action Steps for Business Owners

Identify the principles of persuasion

Spend time understanding the six principles of persuasion and how they work. Identify how these principles can be applied to your business and your marketing and advertising strategies.

Use reciprocity

Use reciprocity by offering something of value to customers in order to encourage them to purchase your products or services. This could be a free trial, a free sample, or some other type of valuable content.

Use scarcity

Use scarcity by highlighting the limited availability of your products or services or by creating a sense of urgency around purchasing. Use language that emphasises the scarcity of your products or services, such as "limited time only" or "while supplies last."

Use authority

Use authority by positioning yourself or your products as being endorsed by experts or by using testimonials from satisfied customers. Highlight any credentials or experience that make you an authority in your field.

Use consistency

Use consistency by asking customers to make a public commitment to your products or services. This could be as simple as asking them to sign up for a newsletter or follow your social media accounts. Once they have made a small commitment, they are more likely to make larger commitments in the future.

Use liking

Use liking by developing relationships with customers, being friendly and approachable, and highlighting similarities between yourself and your customers. Be genuine and authentic in your interactions with customers.

Use social proof

Use social proof by highlighting the popularity of your products or services, using customer reviews and testimonials, and creating a sense of community around your brand. Encourage customers to share their experiences with your products or services on social media and other platforms.

Create a sense of urgency

Create a sense of urgency around purchasing by using language that emphasises the limited availability of your products or services. Use phrases such as "limited time only" or "while supplies last" to create a sense of urgency.

Develop relationships with customers

Focus on developing relationships with customers by being responsive to their needs and concerns. Provide exceptional customer service and go above and beyond to meet their needs.

Use data to inform your strategies

Use data and analytics to track the effectiveness of your persuasion strategies and make adjustments as needed. Use A/B testing and other techniques to test the effectiveness of different strategies and identify areas for improvement.

Conclusion

Influence: The Psychology of Persuasion by Robert Cialdini provides a powerful framework for understanding the psychology of persuasion and how businesses can use it to influence customers. By understanding the six principles of persuasion - reciprocity, scarcity, authority, consistency, liking, and social proof - businesses can develop more effective marketing and advertising strategies, close more sales, and negotiate more effectively. By using language that emphasises scarcity and urgency, developing relationships with customers, and using data to inform their strategies, businesses can apply the principles of persuasion to drive business success.

www.ingramcontent.com/pod-product-compliance
Lightning Source LLC
Chambersburg PA
CBHW052315220526
45472CB00001B/129